Artotype Britton & Rey, S. F.   Inst. Photo. A. P. Flagtor, S. F.

MARKET STREET CABLE RAILWAY, SAN FRANCISCO.

TERMINUS AT FERRY LANDINGS ON THE CITY FRONT, FOOT OF MARKET STREET, SHOWING CARS ARRIVING, TURNING AND DEPARTING.

THE

PACIFIC CABLE RAILWAY COMPANY.

THE SYSTEM OF

WIRE-CABLE RAILWAYS

FOR

CITIES AND TOWNS

AS OPERATED IN

SAN FRANCISCO, LOS ANGELES, CHICAGO, ST. LOUIS, KANSAS CITY,
NEW YORK, CINCINNATI, HOBOKEN, Etc.

SAN FRANCISCO, CAL.

1887.

©2007-2010 Periscope Film LLC
All Rights Reserved
ISBN #978-1-935700-16-6
www.PeriscopeFilm.com

Pacific Cable Railway Company.

INCORPORATED UNDER THE LAWS OF THE STATE OF CALIFORNIA.

OFFICERS.

A. S. HALLIDIE,	*President*
CHAS. F. CROCKER,	*Vice-President*
F. F. LOW,	*Treasurer*
J. L. WILLCUTT,	*Secretary*

DIRECTORS.

LELAND STANFORD,	A. S. HALLIDIE,
F. F. LOW,	C. F. CROCKER,
JOSEPH BRITTON,	J. L. WILLCUTT.

OFFICE OF THE COMPANY:

329 Market Street, — *San Francisco, Cal.*

The National Cable Railway Company.

INCORPORATED UNDER THE LAWS OF THE STATE OF NEW YORK.

OFFICERS.

HENRY L. DAVIS,	*President*
JAMES W. TOWNE,	*Vice-President and Treasurer*
CHAS. R. PARSONS,	*Secretary*

TRUSTEES.

HENRY L. DAVIS,	ELLINGHAM MAYNARD,
JAMES W. TOWNE,	JOSEPH C. WALCOTT,
CHARLES R. PARSONS,	MARTIN B. KLOPP,
WILLIAM C. DAVIS,	FRANK W. WILSON,
ALFRED PECKHAM.	

OFFICE OF THE COMPANY:

140 Nassau Street, Room 25, — *New York, N. Y.*

CONTENTS.

	PAGE
NOTICE AS TO INFRINGEMENT OF PATENT RIGHTS,	5
THE CABLE RAILWAY SYSTEM,	11
LIST OF RAILWAYS CONSTRUCTED UNDER THE PATENTS BELONGING TO THE NATIONAL CABLE RAILWAY CO., AND PACIFIC CABLE RAILWAY CO.,	12
ADVANTAGES OF THE SYSTEM,	14
GENERAL DESCRIPTION OF THE SYSTEM AS IN USE IN SAN FRANCISCO, CAL.:—	
CLAY STREET HILL RAILROAD,	14
SUTTER STREET RAILROAD,	22
CALIFORNIA STREET CABLE RAILROAD,	22
GEARY STREET, PARK, AND OCEAN RAILROAD,	22
PRESIDIO AND FERRIES RAILROAD,	22
MARKET STREET CABLE RAILWAY,	23
POWELL STREET RAILWAY,	31
THE SYSTEM IN OTHER CITIES:—	
CHICAGO CITY RAILWAY,	31
LOS ANGELES CABLE ROADS,	33
OAKLAND CABLE RAILWAY	33
KANSAS CITY AND OTHER CITIES IN THE UNITED STATES,	33
MELBOURNE, AUSTRALIA: GREAT BRITAIN, ETC.,	34
DESCRIPTIVE LIST OF UNITED STATES LETTERS PATENT BELONGING TO THE NATIONAL CABLE RAILWAY CO., AND PACIFIC CABLE RAILWAY CO.,	40
TABULAR STATEMENT OF INFORMATION AS TO CABLE ROADS IN OPERATION,	52
TABLES OF THE COMPARATIVE VALUES OF LAND IN SAN FRANCISCO, SHOWING EFFECT OF CABLE RAILWAY CONSTRUCTION UPON REAL ESTATE,	53

ILLUSTRATIONS.

	PAGE
VIEWS ON THE LINES OF CABLE RAILWAYS IN SAN FRANCISCO:—	
MARKET STREET CABLE RAILWAY—TERMINUS AT FERRY LANDINGS,	Frontispiece
CLAY STREET HILL RAILROAD,	6
SUTTER STREET RAILROAD,	7
CALIFORNIA STREET CABLE RAILROAD,	8
GEARY STREET, PARK AND OCEAN RAILROAD,	9
VIEWS OF MACHINERY, ROAD-BED, CARS, ETC., CLAY ST., GEARY ST., AND PRESIDIO RAILROADS, SAN FRANCISCO,	
ELEVATION OF ENGINE HOUSE—CLAY STREET HILL RAILROAD,	15
PLAN OF ENGINE ROOM, " "	16
CROSS-SECTION OF TUBE, PULLEYS, ETC., "	17
PERSPECTIVE AND SKELETON VIEWS OF GRIP, "	18
ISOMETRICAL VIEW OF ROAD-BED—GEARY STREET RAILROAD,	19
VIEW OF GRIP AND CARRYING FRAME, "	20
SECTION OF ROAD-BED AND DUMMY—PRESIDIO AND FERRIES RAILROAD,	21
VIEWS OF MACHINERY, ROAD-BED, CARS, ETC., MARKET ST. CABLE RAILWAY, SAN FRANCISCO:—	
ISOMETRICAL VIEW OF FOUNDATION PIERS, ROAD-BED AND CAR,	24
FORWARD AND REAR TRUCKS,	25
VIEW OF CAR, TRUCKS AND GRIP,	26
GRIP ON CARS,	27
VIEW OF DRIVING MACHINERY—HAYES STREET BRANCH LINE,	28
ELEVATION OF DRIVING MACHINERY, ANGLE-SHEAVES, ETC., AT MAIN POWER STATION,	29
PLAN OF " " " "	30
VIEWS ON THE LINES OF THE MARKET ST. CABLE RAILWAY, SAN FRANCISCO:—	
ON MARKET STREET AT JUNCTION WITH GEARY STREET,	35
ON MARKET STREET AT JUNCTION WITH MCALLISTER STREET,	36
ON MARKET STREET AT JUNCTION WITH HAYES AND LARKIN STREETS,	37
ON HAIGHT STREET LEADING TO GOLDEN GATE PARK,	38
ON HAIGHT STREET AT PARK TERMINUS	39
PROFILES OF STREET GRADES,	50-51
VIEW OF CHICAGO CITY RAILWAY,	54
GRIP ON CARS OF "	32
MAP OF SAN FRANCISCO, SHOWING THE CABLE ROADS IN THAT CITY,	55-57

NOTICE.

By various Letters Patent, as hereafter appears, the Government of the United States granted to the persons therein named and their assigns. the exclusive right to make, vend and use the inventions therein described and claimed throughout the United States and the Territories thereof.

These Letters Patent have now been acquired by The National Cable Railway Company (of New York), and the Pacific Cable Railway Company (of California). They include all of the essential or important inventions relating to wire-cable street railways as constructed and operated in the United States, England, Australia and New Zealand: the earliest and broadest as well as the latest and most detailed inventions are covered by them. The inventions secured by these Letters Patent, therefore, constitute the basis or groundwork of what is known as the wire-cable railway system—being the only system in practical use in constructing cable railways in this or any foreign country, and increasing experience fully demonstrates the absolute necessity for their employment wherever public improvements of this character are introduced. Although some short experimental roads have been built on principles or pretended "systems" designed to avoid the necessity of using these patents, the impracticability of roads so built has led to their abandonment.

The Companies named are fully assured as to all of the rights claimed by them. They realize the importance of these inventions and, while determined to suffer no infringement upon their rights, it is their policy and will continue to be so, to encourage the building and operation of cable railways, by licenses and special grants of privileges and interests under these patents on fair and liberal terms.

Nevertheless for their own protection, and for the information of all whom it may concern, *notice is hereby given* that the *unauthorized* construction or operation of street railways worked by a moving endless cable in an underground slotted tube on the principle of the cable railways now being operated in various cities of the United States (irrespective of any modifications in the details of construction) is an infringement upon the patent rights above referred to, and in case of any such infringement said Companies are and will be entitled to all receipts and profits derived from the use of all or any of the inventions covered by the said Letters Patent, as well as to damages therefor. To secure these, and to prevent further infringement, they have determined to vigorously prosecute actions for damages and mesne profits, and, wherever necessary, to obtain injunctions against all persons or corporations offending in this regard.

THE NATIONAL CABLE RAILWAY COMPANY,
140 Nassau Street, New York, N. Y.

PACIFIC CABLE RAILWAY COMPANY,
329 Market Street, San Francisco, Cal.

CLAY STREET HILL WIRE ROPE RAIL ROAD,

ASCENDING AN INCLINE OF ONE FOOT IN SIX. — THE FIRST CABLE ROAD CONSTRUCTED.

SUTTER STREET WIRE ROPE RAIL ROAD.
THIS FORMERLY A HORSE ROAD, WAS CHANGED TO A WIRE ROPE ROAD.

CALIFORNIA STREET WIRE ROPE RAIL ROAD.
STEEPEST GRADE 18 FEET IN 100 FEET.

GEARY STREET WIRE ROPE RAIL ROAD.

A PORTION OF THE TRACK OF THIS COMPANY WAS FORMERLY AND IS NOW USED BY THE HORSE CARS OF OTHER COMPANIES.

PACIFIC CABLE RAILWAY COMPANY.

THE NATIONAL CABLE RAILWAY COMPANY.

THE SYSTEM OF CABLE RAILWAYS

AS OPERATED BY STREET RAILWAY COMPANIES IN

SAN FRANCISCO, CHICAGO, KANSAS CITY, ST. LOUIS, NEW YORK, OAKLAND, LOS ANGELES, HOBOKEN, CINCINNATI, ETC.

The wire-cable system of street railways was invented and first put into use in the United States. In the year 1873 a wire-cable road was constructed and operated in the City of San Francisco, California, which was followed by the construction of several other cable roads in that city, and as the merits and advantages of the system—as the most practical method yet discovered of operating street railways—have become known, it has been gradually extended to other cities in the United States, and by the enterprise of the inventor and one of the principal patentees has been introduced and is now in operation in London, Melbourne and Sydney, and he is now making arrangements for its introduction into the principal cities of Europe.

Letters Patent were in the year 1872 issued by the Government of the United States to the inventor for devices relating to cable railways, and in the years following a number of most important improvements and inventions were made by himself and others for which patents were also granted. They include the United States Letters Patent granted to Hallidie, Eppelsheimer, Casebolt, Root, Paine, and others, and broadly cover the principle of constructing and operating wire-cable railways, being bottom patents, and embrace all the essential parts of a cable railway and the cable grips in use in the United States, and it is under these patents that the wire-cable railways have been built which are now in successful operation in San Francisco, Chicago, Los Angeles, Kansas City, St. Louis, Oakland, Hoboken and elsewhere. All of these patents have been acquired by the National and Pacific Cable Railway Companies for the entire United States and Territories; such ownership being divided between the Companies by the 106th degree of longitude west from Greenwich, the right for the territory east of that line belonging to the National Cable Railway Company, while the Pacific Cable Railway Company is the owner of the patents for the territory west of that meridian, and by the concentration of them under one general ownership the patent problem is greatly simplified.

A descriptive account of these Letters Patent will be found at page 57.

Parties desiring to construct cable railways will find it to their interest to secure a license, from either the National Cable Railway Company or Pacific Cable Railway Company, for the use of all the inventions covered by these patents, for by this means they will not only avoid litigation at an expense insignificant in comparison with the outlay necessary for the construction of such roads, but will obtain the right to use the best and most approved methods of construction and operation —the result of years of experience.

Under these Patents the following wire-cable street railways have been constructed or are now in operation by virtue of rights and licenses granted to their owners, viz:

Railway	Location	Year
Clay Street Hill Railroad,	San Francisco, Cal.	1873
Sutter Street Railroad,	" " "	1876
California Street Cable Railroad,	" " "	1878
Geary Street, Park and Ocean Railroad,	" " "	1880
Presidio and Ferries Railroad,	" " "	1881
Market Street Cable Railway,	" " "	1883
Powell Street Railway,*	" " "	1887
Chicago City Railway,	Chicago, Ill.	1882
New York and Brooklyn Bridge Cable Railway,	Brooklyn, N. Y.	1883
Kansas City Cable Railway,	Kansas City Mo.	1885
Metropolitan Street Railway,	" " "	1886
Grand Avenue Cable Railway,	" " "	1887
Peoples' Passenger Railway,*	" " "	1887
St. Louis Cable and Western Railway,	St. Louis, Mo.	1886
Citizens' Railway,	" " "	1887
Second Street Cable Railroad,	Los Angeles, Cal.	1885
Temple Street Cable Railway,	" " "	1886
Oakland Cable Railway,	Oakland, "	1886
N. Hudson Co. Railway (Elevated),	Hoboken, N. J.	1886
Omaha Cable Tramway,*	Omaha, Neb.	1887

* Near completion.

In addition to the foregoing, the construction of other cable railways under these Patents is either proceeding or is intended by their projectors at an early date, as the following will show:

The Portland Cable Railway Co. of Portland, Or., has contracted for the purchase of the right to use the patents of these Companies and is about to commence building the first cable railway in that city.

The Missouri Railroad Co. of St. Louis has obtained a license for the use of these patents, and has commenced converting its railway, previously a horse road, into a cable railway.

In Kansas City two additional cable street railway companies have been organized and have purchased the right to use these patents in the construction of their roads.

The Denver Cable Railway Co. has secured an option for the purchase of the right to use these patents in the construction of cable railways in Denver, Col.

The St. Paul City Railway Co. holds a license for the use of these patents in the construction of its cable road, for which purpose the material is now on the ground and everything ready for the commencement of work.

Negotiations are also pending with other street railway companies for the use of the patents of these Companies in the construction of cable railways.

THE ENDLESS WIRE-CABLE SYSTEM,

the successful introduction and continued operation of which as an element of motor power in the propulsion of street railway cars, marks an era as full of possibilities as any that have preceded it through the important inventions that have contributed so much to the comfort, convenience and necessities of the present generation—is adapted to all kinds of service, equally for crowded thoroughfares and level grades as for streets which are so steep as to make the use of horses impossible; while in carrying capacity it is unlimited in cases where an increase is required.

The desirability of the more elevated portions of a city for residences, and the limited street car service supplied by animal power to such localities, together with the necessity for a more economical and rapid method of operating street railways, have for many years attracted the attention of railway managers and mechanical engineers throughout the world, and of the various methods which have been introduced and experimented upon, the most practicable one yet found is that of the wire-cable system.

The concentration at one point remote from observation of the entire motor power of an extended line of railway; the movement of any number of cars at any desired rate of speed, at any intervals of time without noise, fire or smoke, without a locomotive of any kind, either steam, compressed air, or electric; the easy ascent and descent of grades, however steep or abrupt; the ready facility of adding to or diminishing the number of cars in the exact ratio of the hourly demand; and all this at three-fifths the cost of any other method—is what the cable system claims to have completely demonstrated.

The system consists simply of an endless wire rope placed in a tube (having a narrow slot from $\frac{1}{2}$ to $\frac{3}{4}$ inch wide), beneath the surface and between the rails, maintained in its position by means of sheaves, wheels or rollers. The rope is kept continuously in motion by a stationary steam-engine at either end of the line, or at any convenient point between the two extremes.

A griping attachment at the end of a vertical steel rod connected with the car, and passing through the narrow slot in the tube, transmits the motion of the cable to the car. The speed at which the car moves is determined by the rapidity of the cable, and this is regulated by the revolutions of the driving wheel at the stationary engine. The cable is grasped and released at pleasure, and the movement of the car controlled with perfect ease by one man. The car or cars (there may be any number used together) start smoothly without shock or jar, and are stopped instantly at any point more readily than a horse car, and hence are less liable to accidents. The system can be adapted to any grade or curvature, even to turning the corner of a street at acute angles of limited radius. There are no impediments whatever to the use of the system, either of soil, climate or temperature.

THE ADVANTAGES OF THE SYSTEM

may be summarized as follows:

1. The steepest grades are as easily worked as levels.
2. The cars may be stopped instantly at any point on the line, and started with promptness and ease.
3. The speed is uniform, and any rate may be established that is desired.
4. The method of working is noiseless and even, and unaccompanied by any annoyance whatever.
5. Perfect cleanliness of the track is secured, an important sanitary element in the system.
6. An unlimited capacity of increase at any time an increased carrying capacity may be required.
7. Perfect freedom from snow blockade, as the power is sufficient at all times to remove the snow as fast as it falls.
8. A simple and economical administration, unattended with unforeseen and unexpected emergencies.

The wire-cable system of car propulsion was first applied to street railways in San Francisco, where the steep gradients of some of the streets rendered the use of horses expensive or impossible, and by its complete adaptation to the requirements of the public soon became attended with great and unqualified success.

A map of the City of San Francisco is appended, for the purpose of showing the lines of route of the various cable railways in that city and their relative position to each other.

The system was matured by Mr. Andrew S. Hallidie, and by him and his associates first put into practical use by the construction of the Clay Street Hill Railroad in San Francisco, in August, 1873, since which time the road has been constantly running, and has been found to answer all requirements.

A GENERAL DESCRIPTION OF THE SYSTEM,

as in use on the CLAY STREET HILL RAILROAD OF SAN FRANCISCO, will best explain the *modus operandi*.

Clay Street is a central street in that city, and for a number of blocks near the lower terminus of the road is very densely populated. The street is only 49 feet wide from house to house, and between the sidewalks is occupied by two lines of gas pipe, one line of water pipe, a street sewer, and at the cross streets by water cisterns. The lower terminus of the road is at the intersection of Kearny and Clay Streets. The summit of the hill is 307 feet above Kearny Street. The road has a double track, and is 5197 feet long; the rope runs into the engine-house at Leavenworth Street. The ascending grades are as follows (see profile of street grades, page 67): From Kearny to Dupont, 45 feet; from Dupont to Stockton, 45 feet; from Stockton to Powell, 62 feet; from Powell to Mason, 40 feet; from Mason to Taylor, 48 feet; from Taylor to Jones, 67 feet. Then the grade descends, as follows: Jones to Leavenworth, 15 feet; Leavenworth to Hyde, 50 feet; Hyde to Larkin, 50 feet; Larkin to Polk, 45 feet; and then there is an ascent of 15 feet from Polk Street to Van Ness Avenue. The distance between each street is $412\frac{1}{2}$ feet. Clay Street runs at right angles to the above streets, which have widths varying from 45 feet to 68 feet 9 inches. All the street crossings are level. The steepest grade is 1 in $6\frac{15}{100}$.

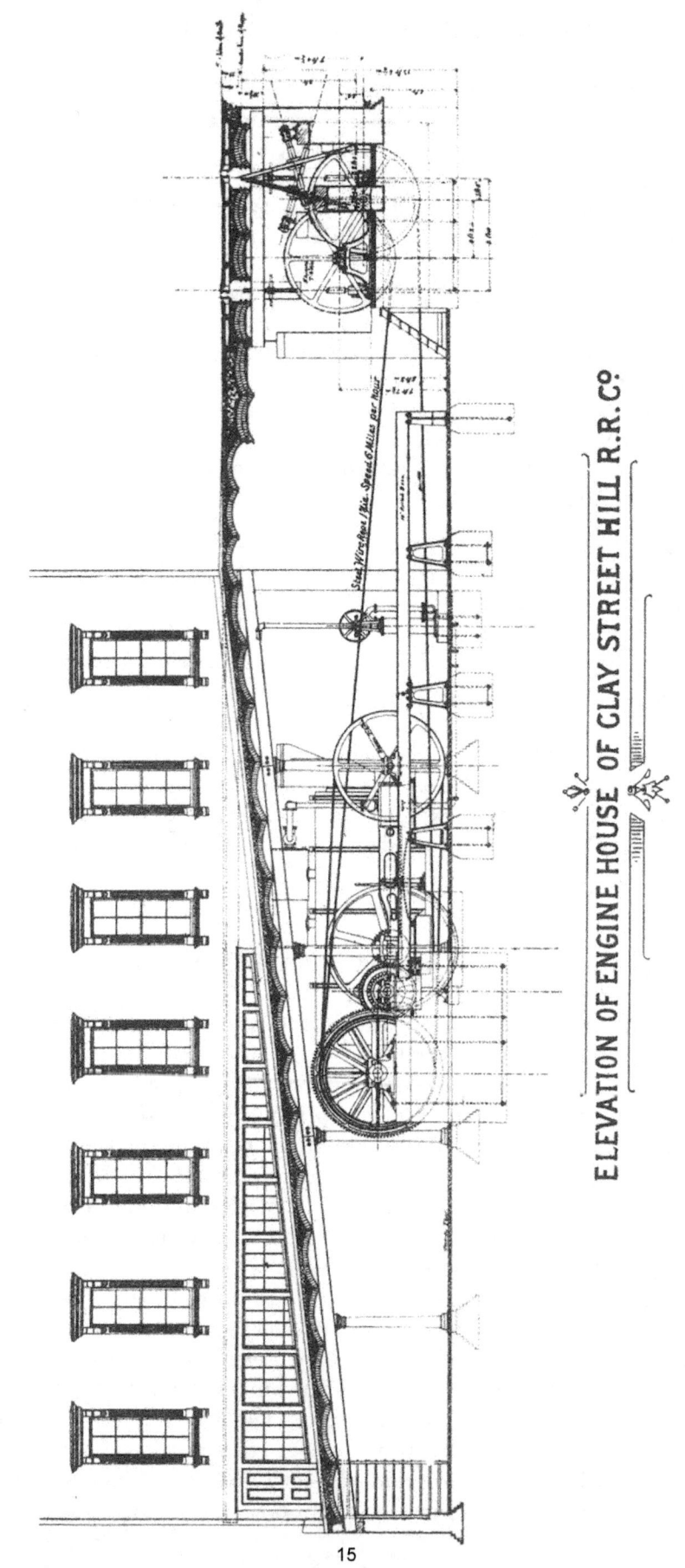

ELEVATION OF ENGINE HOUSE OF CLAY STREET HILL R.R. CO.

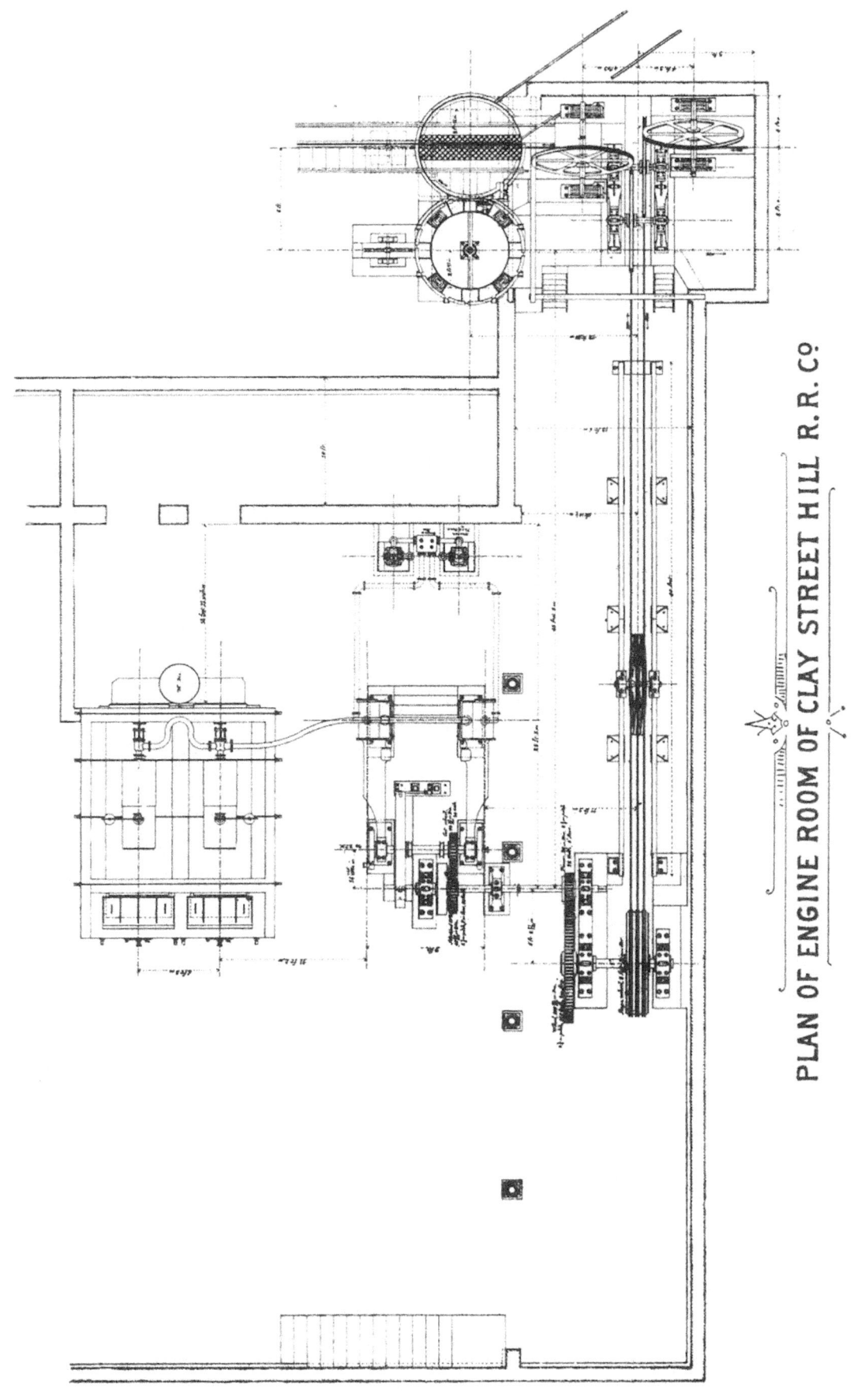

PLAN OF ENGINE ROOM OF CLAY STREET HILL R.R. CO.

An endless steel wire rope three inches in circumference, 11,000 feet long, is stretched the whole distance, lying in iron tubes, supported every 39 feet on 11-inch sheaves. This rope is supported at every change of angle at the lower crossings on sheaves four feet in diameter, passing around a horizontal sheave eight feet in diameter at the lower end of the line, and at the engine-house, or power station, around two angle sheaves, each eight feet in diameter, which lead the rope on the driving pulleys, also eight feet in diameter, which are driven by one 14 x 28 engine. The steam is furnished by one boiler, 16 feet x 54 inches, using 3700 pounds of coal per day. There are also duplicate engine and boiler, which are held in reserve.

Fig. 1.

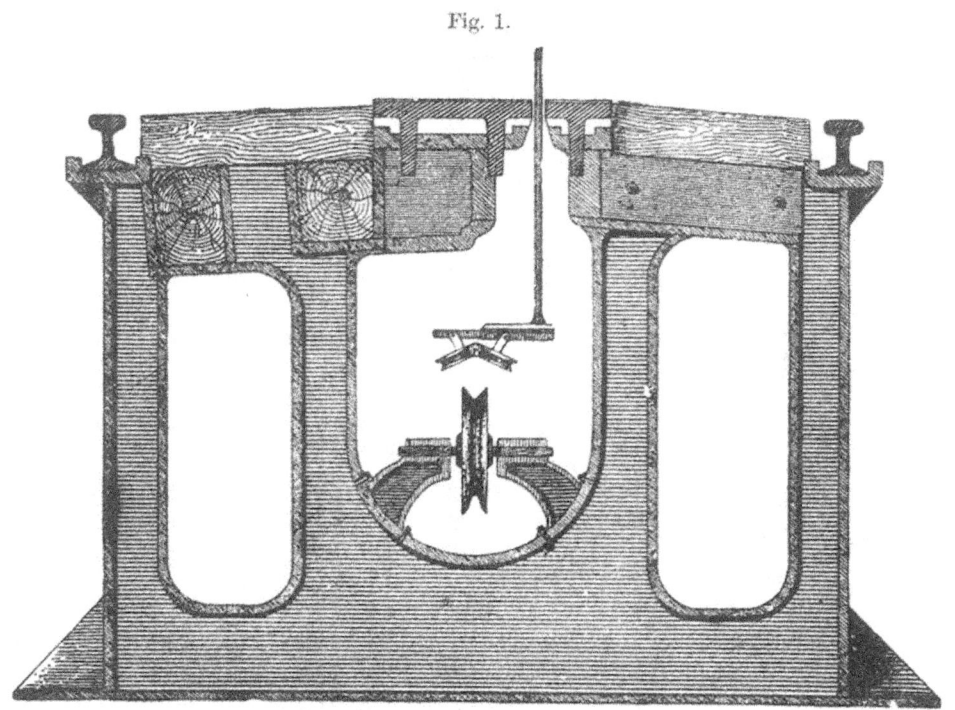

CROSS-SECTION OF TUBE, PULLEYS, ETC., CLAY STREET HILL R. R., SAN FRANCISCO, WESTERLY FROM LEAVENWORTH STREET.

In addition to the sheaves that support the rope in the tubes, at the upper side of each crossing where the incline makes an angle upwards, there are sheaves in the tubes that keep the rope down and from striking the upper part of the tube.

There is an opening in the upper side of the tube. This opening runs the entire length of each tube, forming a long slot three-fourths of an inch wide on the surface of the street. This slot is not immediately over the centre of the tube, but on one side, to keep sand and drift from falling on the rope, and enable the foot of the griping attachment to pass by and under the upper sheaves, and over the lower sheaves in the tube.

The connection between the cars on the street and the traveling rope is made by means of this griping attachment, as shown in Figs. 2 and 3. The cars on this road are made to seat 14 passengers and the dummy 16, but frequently as many as 44 have ridden in the car and 26 on the dummy—70 in all. It is true they were crowded, but this is always the case on holidays. The grip-car, or "dummy," with the griping attachment, is attached firmly to the passenger car, so that there can be no danger of accident. The dummy and car are amply provided with brakes. In addition to the usual car-brake, there is another attachment, which forces a broad band of wood down on each track immediately under the car.

The road has a gauge of 3½ feet. An ordinary 30-pound steel T rail is used, which is set flush with the street. The stretching arrangement at the lower end keeps a constant strain on the rope under all circumstances.

Fig. 2.

Fig. 3.

PERSPECTIVE VIEW OF GRIP USED ON
CLAY ST. HILL RAILROAD,
SAN FRANCISCO.

SKELETON VIEW OF GRIP USED ON
CLAY ST. HILL RAILROAD,
SAN FRANCISCO.

By referring to the drawings the system will be more clearly understood.

Fig. 1, page 23, is a cross-section of tube, pulleys, etc., on the Clay Street Hill Railroad, westerly from Leavenworth Street.

Figs. 2 and 3, page 24, give perspective and skeleton views of grip used on Clay Street Hill Railroad.

On page 25 is an isometrical view of the road-bed of the Geary Street, Park and Ocean Railroad, San Francisco, and carrying frame and wheels of the dummy or grip car, the spring body and a portion of the tube being removed to show the griping device attached to the rope.

On page 27 is a view of the grip and carrying frame in use on the Geary Street Railroad.

On page 29 is a section of the road-bed and dummy of the Presidio and Ferries Railroad, San Francisco, with griping attachment.

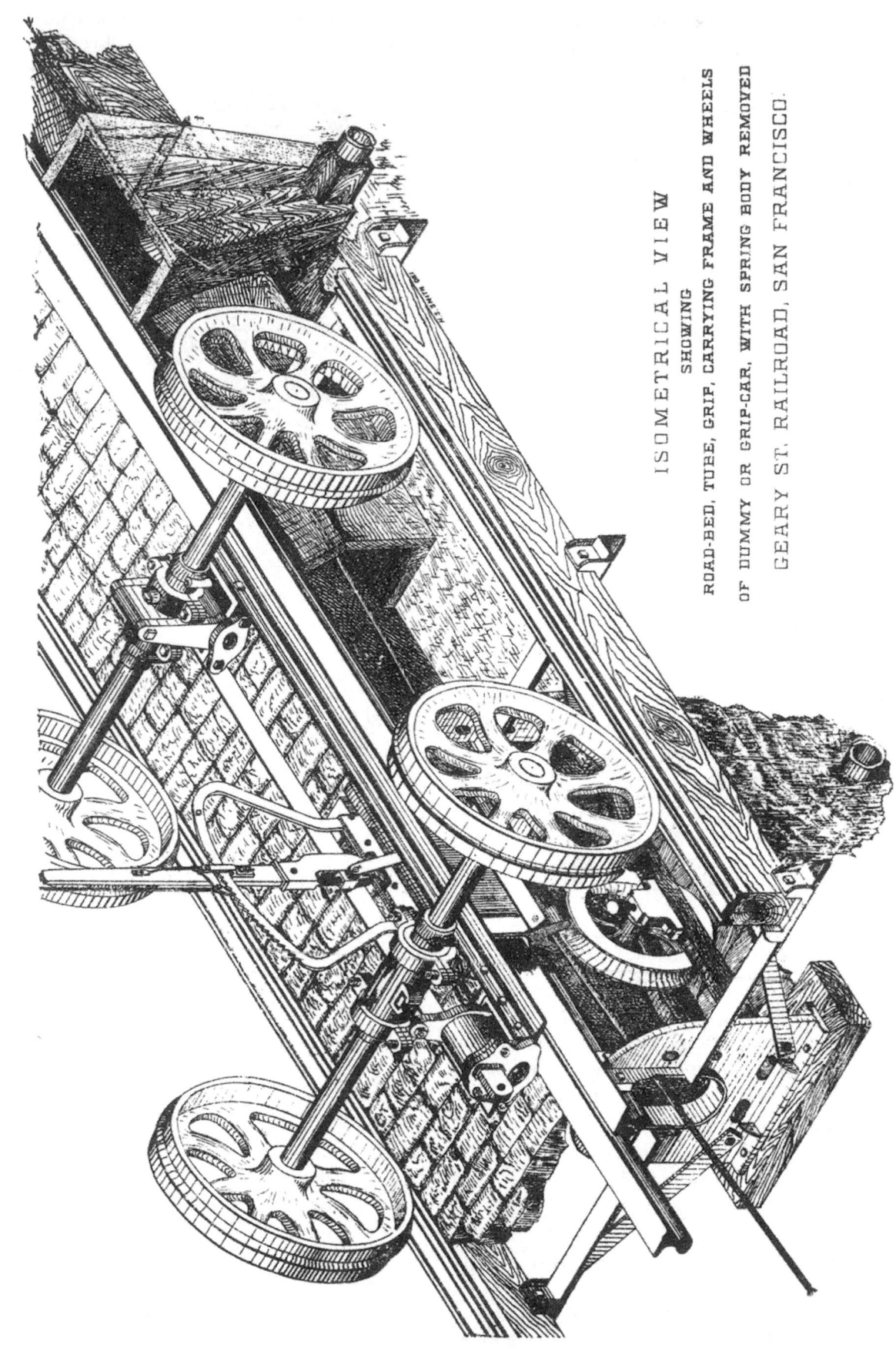

ISOMETRICAL VIEW
SHOWING
ROAD-BED, TUBE, GRIP, CARRYING FRAME AND WHEELS
OF DUMMY OR GRIP-CAR, WITH SPRING BODY REMOVED
GEARY ST. RAILROAD, SAN FRANCISCO.

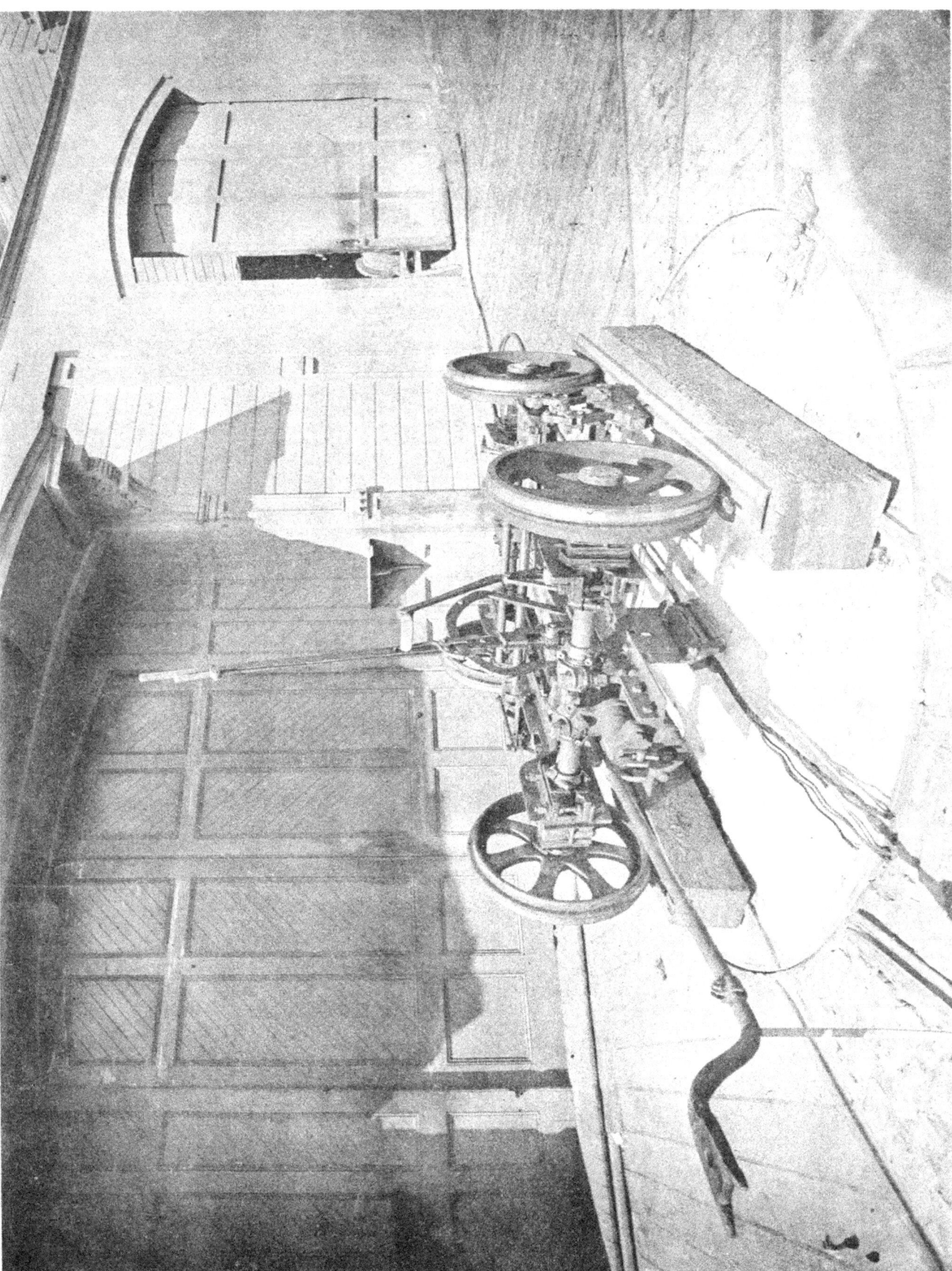

GEARY STREET RAILROAD.

VIEW OF GRIP, CARRYING FRAME OF DUMMY AND RAIL-BRAKE.

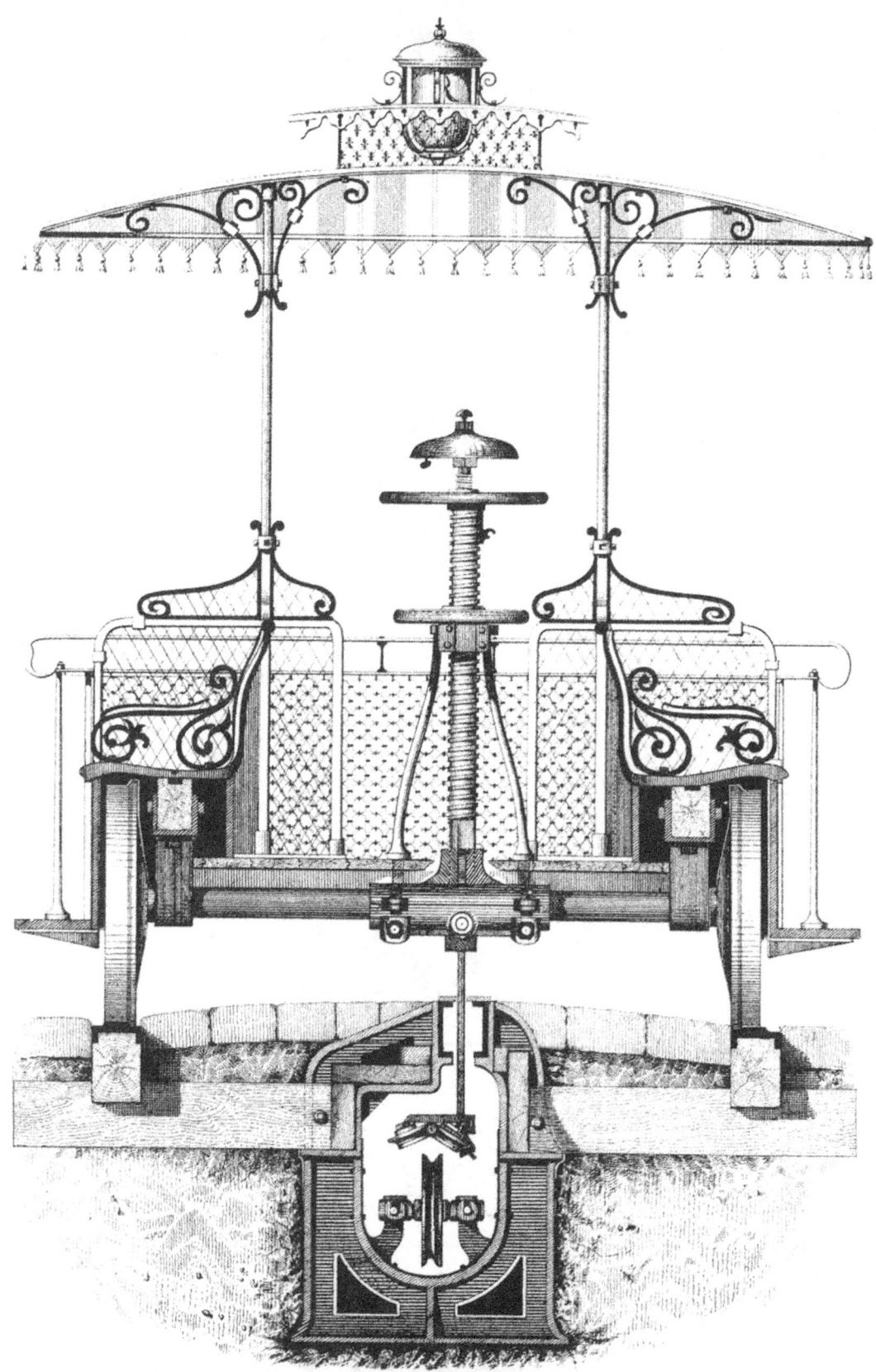

SECTION OF ROAD-BED AND DUMMY

PRESIDIO AND FERRIES RAILROAD,
SAN FRANCISCO.

The SUTTER STREET RAILROAD COMPANY, whose lines had for many years been unsatisfactorily operated with animal power, commenced to change its system from a horse road to a wire-cable railway in 1876, and by the end of the year 1879 the Company had reconstructed nearly its entire road on this system. This Company now has over 21,000 feet (or about four miles) of double track operated on this system. The gauge of the road is 5 feet, and its greatest elevation (at Gough Street) is 207 feet above its initial point.

The main cable line is on Sutter Street, and is 13,200 feet long. A branch cable road, at right angles to the main line, runs on Larkin and Ninth Streets, and is 7890 feet long. This latter road runs across two other cable roads, viz: the Market Street and Geary Street railroads.

The griping attachment used by this Company is somewhat different in construction from that on the Clay Street road, although involving the same principles. The motion of the griping jaws is vertical instead of horizontal, and it takes and releases the rope sideways, instead of beneath, as with the Clay Street grip, and in order to run on to or off from the rope at the termini of the cable road, the track and slot diverge from or converge to the line of the rope. Levers are used for operating the jaws instead of the screw.

The CALIFORNIA STREET CABLE RAILROAD commenced running April, 1878. Its length is over 12,000 feet of double track, and in that distance it passes over two elevations, the heights being 265 feet and 245 feet above the initial point at Kearny Street, the valley between being 160 feet above base, or 125 feet above the initial point. The gauge is $3\frac{1}{2}$ feet, same as the Clay Street road.

The grip employed is worked by a lever, and like that of the Sutter Street road, takes the rope sideways.

The GEARY STREET, PARK AND OCEAN RAILROAD runs over a comparatively level street, and through one of the most central and populous streets of the city. It was completed and commenced running February, 1880.

The gauge of the road is 5 feet, and its length is 12,500 feet of double track, in which distance it passes over two elevations, 120 and 200 feet above base, respectively, and attains a third elevation at its westerly terminus of 248 feet above base—its starting point at Kearny Street being 35 feet above base, and the two intermediate valleys being 117 and 105 feet, respectively, above base.

The tube is constructed of cast-iron yokes, and the space inside the tubes is much less than that on any other road, the cable carrying wheels being in pits, each having a drainage pipe. The grip is worked by levers. It is vertical in its motion, and takes the rope from above, the griping jaws being immediately under the slot.

The PRESIDIO AND FERRIES RAILROAD commenced running in October, 1880. It has a five-foot gauge; and nearly 11,000 feet of double track. It ascends one hill 246 feet above its initial point in a distance of 5,000 feet. The engine is located on the summit of the hill, about midway between the termini, and about 700 feet from the summit is a very heavy grade of 78 feet in $412\frac{1}{2}$, or 1 in $5\frac{3}{10}$. The road is built very substantially, with cast-iron sections or yokes connected by rolled channel iron and sheet iron.

The grip is the same as the one used on the Clay Street road, although made heavier, to conform to the heavier grades and rolling stock.

All of these roads were constructed under patents among those belonging to the National and Pacific Cable Railway Companies.

The **MARKET STREET CABLE RAILWAY** is the most extensive, and with one exception the latest of the cable roads in San Francisco. Its main line extends in a southwesterly direction from the water-front and ferry landings through Market Street, the greatest thoroughfare in that city, having a length of $3\frac{1}{4}$ miles with a width of 120 feet. Four branch lines diverge at intervals, the principal one to the south towards the Mission hills, and the three other branches to the west at an angle of about 35 degrees from the main line, terminating at the Golden Gate Park. The cars of the branch lines run over the main line from the points of divergence to the terminus at the water-front. The road is a double track railway with a 4-foot $8\frac{1}{2}$ inch gauge.

The lengths of the main line and branches, operated by cable, are as follows:

Main line on Market Street (double track),	2.2	miles
Branch line on Valencia Street " "	1.9	"
*Branch line on Market and Castro Sts. " "	1.9	"
Branch line on Haight Street " "	1.8	"
Branch line on Hayes Street " "	2.1	"
Branch line on McAllister Street " "	2.4	"
Total, - -	12.3	"

though the total number of miles operated by the various lines through running over the main line on Market Street is nearly twenty.

The old Market Street Railroad, composed of the main line and the Valencia Street Branch, was the pioneer line of the city and had been operated as a horse-car line for 16 years. It was converted into a cable road and two of the additional branches were constructed in 1883; another branch (Hayes Street line) was added during the year 1886, and the latest branch, (the Castro Street line) is now in course of construction.

The three westerly branch lines run through elevated portions of the city, which from the facilities acquired through the construction of these roads, are rapidly increasing in population. On account of the steep grades (which on Haight and Hayes Streets are 51 and 60 feet in a distance of $412\frac{1}{2}$ feet), they could not well be operated by other than mechanical methods, and the cable system was especially adapted to the purpose. The same remark applies to the latest branch on Castro Street, now under construction, running to the south.

In the construction of this road, its owners were able to profit by the experience of the builders of other cable roads and also to avail themselves of the most recent methods and improvements used in the construction and operation of cable railways.

The foundation for the road-bed and track rests upon concrete piers extending to a depth of 10 feet or more below the surface of the street. These piers have a width of five feet and are 16 inches thick, and are placed about nine feet apart.

The track and tube of this road form a single rigid structure by connecting the rails and slot-irons by yokes, and uniting the whole by employing concrete. The main tie or yoke connecting the opposite rails is formed of old railroad T rail, bent in proper shape head down. It embraces the tube, and has fastened to the ends suitable chairs or plates, to which the rails are secured. From the lower part of the curved yoke extend upward two supports for the slot-irons. The lower ends of these are sufficiently separated to form the necessary width for the tube. Tie-rods

---

*In course of construction and will be in operation during the present year.

connect these supports with the main yokes through the chairs. The two rails, slot-irons and yoke are then all connected rigidly together as one. These yokes are placed every three feet along the length of the road. The rails and slot-irons being connected in the same structure, all the parts are maintained in their relative position. Whatever may occur to alter the place of one has no effect, unless the change is sufficient to affect the whole structure. The slot which is $\frac{7}{8}$ of an inch wide is of steel and is laid $1\frac{1}{2}$ inches higher than the track rail, so as to keep out sand and water, and is placed one inch and a half to the left of the centre of the tube. The paving between the slot and track rail consists of stone blocks. (See Fig. 4.)

Fig. 4.

ISOMETRICAL VIEW OF FOUNDATION PIERS, ROAD-BED AND CAR,
MARKET ST. CABLE RAILWAY, SAN FRANCISCO.

In its construction the Market Street Cable Railway thus became the most thorough and substantial of any cable road ever built.

The cars used on this road are different from those on the earlier cable roads. Instead of the dummy being a separate vehicle, the cars and dummies are made in one, the main portion of the car being enclosed and the forward portion open, having a roof supported by ornamental posts—the entire car being 34 feet long, over all. These cars have carried upwards of 130 passengers at a time, and the improvements are covered by a patent which is among those belonging to the National and Pacific Cable Railway Companies. The car is supported on two four-wheel trucks having a pivot or swivel as on steam railroad coaches; the details of the device being shown in Figs. 5 and 6, page 34. The rear truck carries the track-brake which is between the wheels on each side. In addition there are the usual wheel-brakes. The forward truck carries the grip and brake-levers. A rod connects the rock-shaft of the track-brakes with the hand lever on the forward truck. By the use of these trucks the cars turn the curves easily and ride without jolt. The brakes used on cable roads are very important factors in the system. On this road, particularly, running at a rapid speed and through a crowded thoroughfare, it is necessary to have the brake-gear very efficient, in order that sudden stops can be made.

Fig. 5.

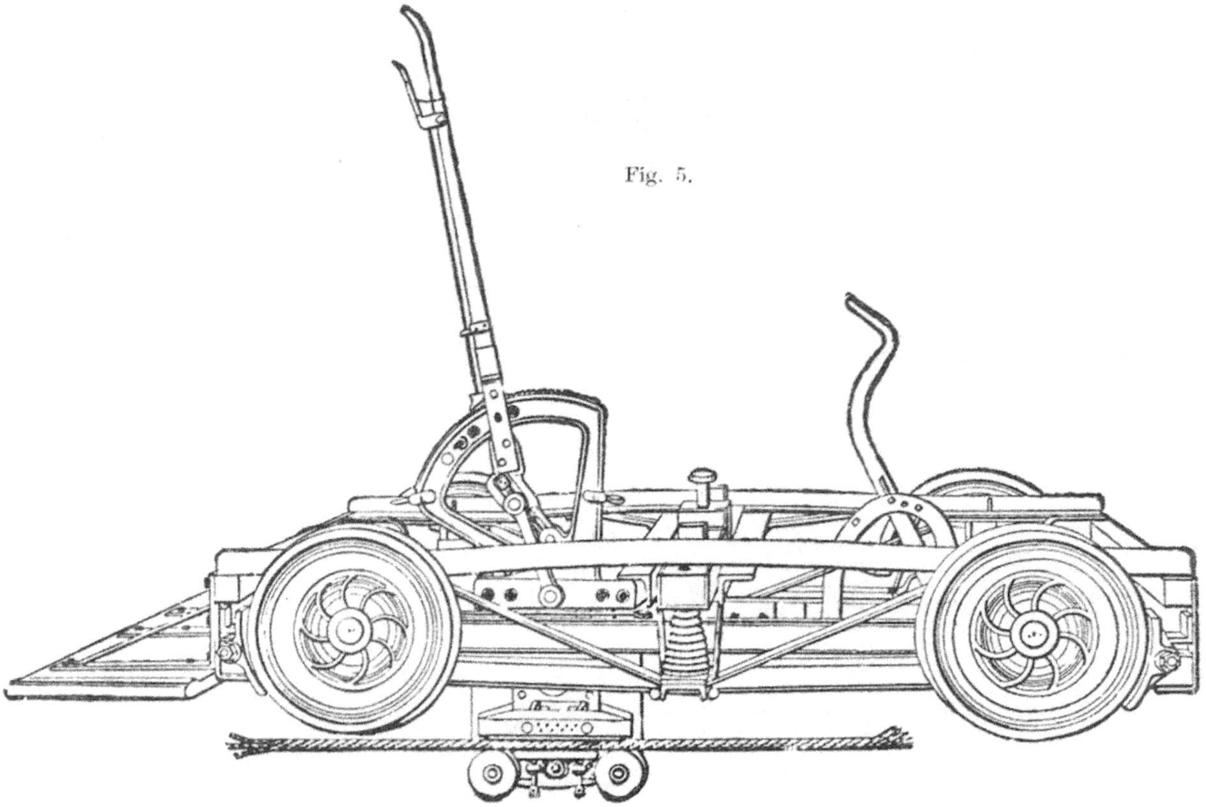

ROOT'S PATENT FORWARD TRUCK, WITH GRIP, BRAKE LEVER AND FENDER.

Fig. 6.

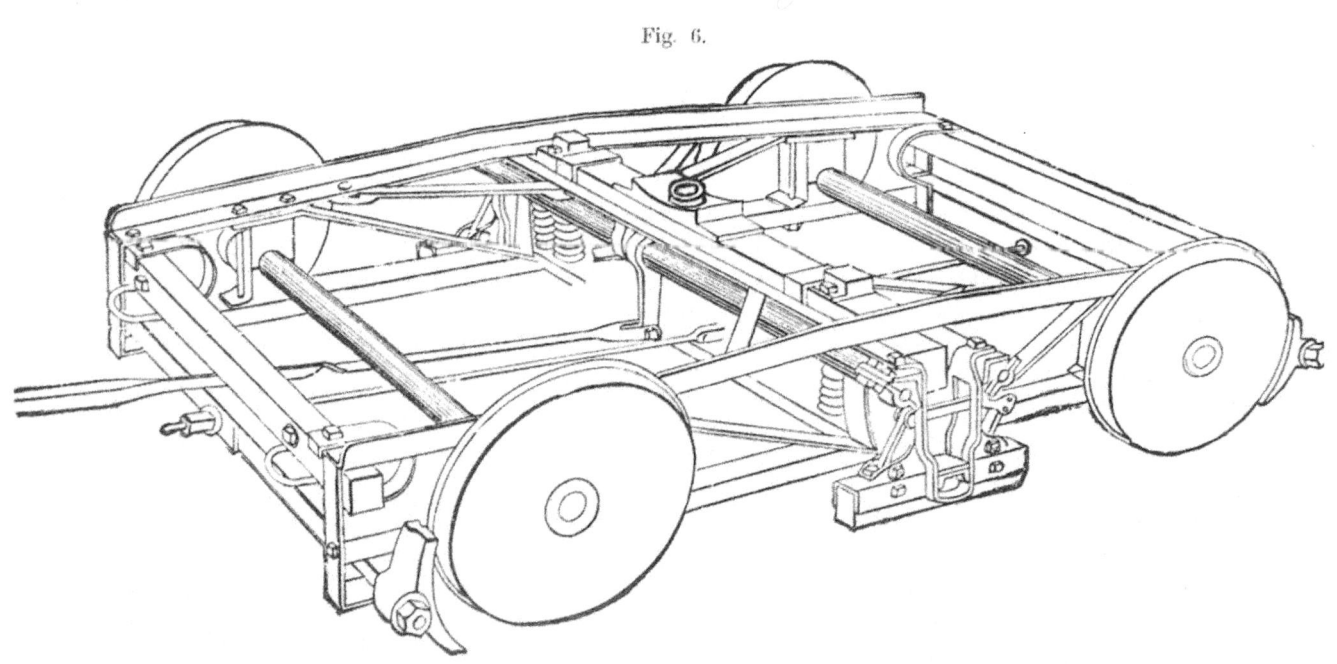

ROOT'S PATENT REAR TRUCK, SHOWING TRACK-BRAKE.

TRUCKS USED ON THE CARS OF THE MARKET STREET CABLE RAILWAY, SAN FRANCISCO.

MARKET STREET CABLE RAILWAY, SAN FRANCISCO.
VIEW OF COMBINATION CAR SHOWING TRUCKS AND GRIP REMOVED.

The grip in use on this road is worked by a lever and is similar to that used on the California Street Railroad, the patent for which belongs to these Companies. It is formed of two frames, one sliding inside the other. The outer one is secured to the grip-bar on the forward truck by bolts, and carries the lower jaw, while the inner frame which slides up and down upon the outer one, carries the upper jaw, the quadrant, the operating lever and adjusting mechanism, and is held in place by guide plates extending across the inside frame, and between which it slides. The frame carrying the jaws passes through the slot directly down alongside the cable, without offset. The grip-bar on which these parts are mounted is secured and supported by a frame on the running gear or truck, and not on the car itself. The car body therefore can be mounted on springs without any of the spring motion being imparted to the grip and through it to the cable. In the way in which this grip is arranged all the parts liable to get out of order are accessible, and it is not necessary to provide pits in which to examine them. The drawing, Fig. 7, shows the construction of the grip.

Fig. 7.

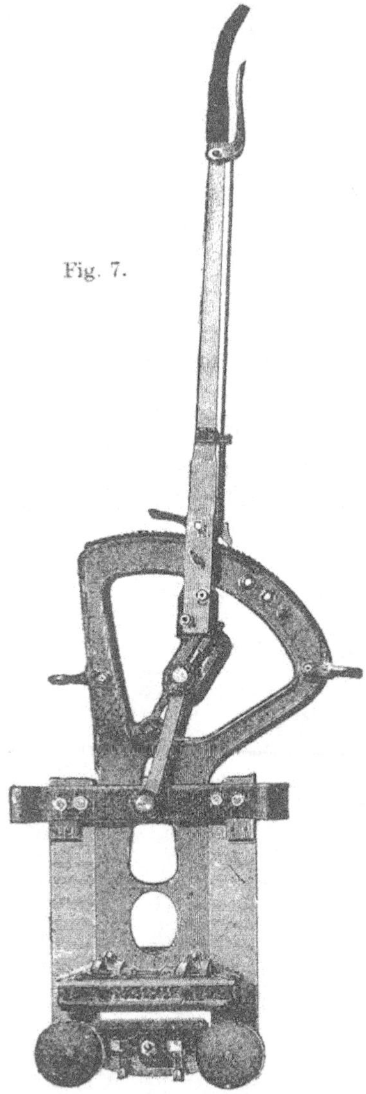

When the car is at a stand-still the cable passes along over the chilled-iron grooved rollers at each end of the lower die. The lever operating the grip is then inclined forward. When the gripman desires to start the car, he draws the hand lever back. This action moves the inner frame downward, carrying with it the upper jaw or die. This die consists of a piece of brass secured in the lower end of the sliding part. The lower die is a shorter piece of brass fitted lengthwise between the two rollers. This is arranged with set screws to be raised to take up wear. The upper die is longer than the lower, and as it is forced down by the inner frame it rests on the moving cable, and pushes or presses it tight on the rollers before pressing it on the lower die. Gradual motion is thus imparted to the car, without jerk or jar. A still further downward motion of the upper die forces the rope or cable on to the lower die, the cable being thus held tightly between the dies. A reverse motion of the lever raises the frame and upper die, and releases the cable and allows it to run through freely without imparting any motion to the car. The action of the brakes then stops the car.

GRIP USED ON
MARKET ST. CABLE RAILWAY,
SAN FRANCISCO,
AND ON RAILWAYS IN
ST. LOUIS, KANSAS CITY, ETC.

The heavy traffic and the great length of the cables on these lines have rendered necessary the use of cables $1\frac{1}{4}$ inches in diameter, which are larger than those first used. Their weight is about $2\frac{1}{2}$ lbs. per foot. The rope runs 21 hours per day at a speed of about 8 miles per hour, the rate of speed for the cars including stoppages being about $7\frac{1}{2}$ miles per hour. Every 30 feet along the road is a grooved supporting pulley 15 inches in diameter over the flanges. These pulleys form the carriers for the rope. Over each pulley is a removable plate 12 x 16 inches, so constructed as to be readily

Fig. 8.

VIEW OF DRIVING MACHINERY, HAYES STREET BRANCH POWER STATION,
MARKET STREET CABLE RAILWAY, SAN FRANCISCO.
Union Iron Works, S. F., Builders.

taken up for oiling the pulley and cleaning the rope way; and at the same time to be secure in its place and to form no obstruction to traffic.

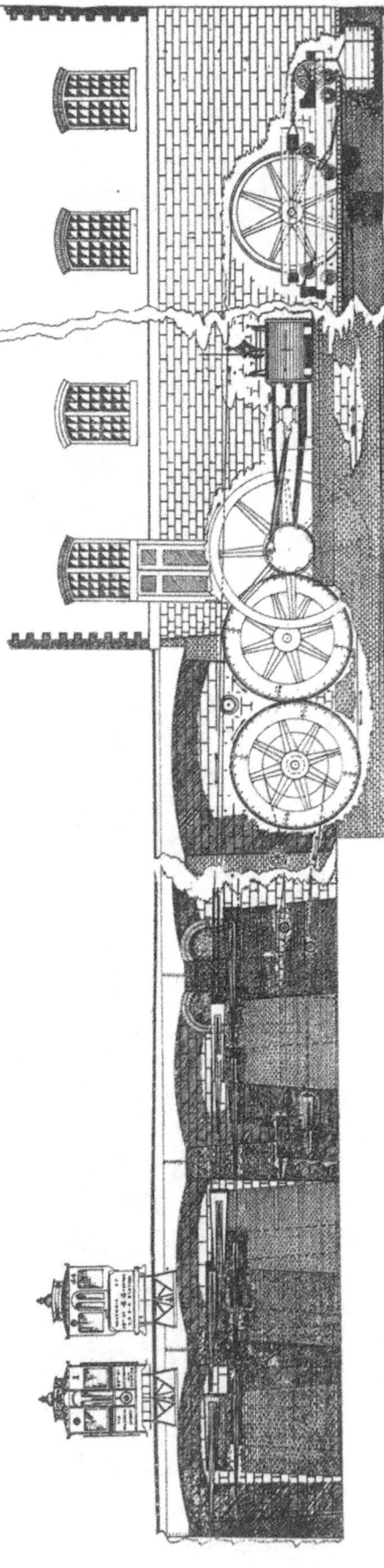

ELEVATION OF THE
DRIVING MACHINERY, ANGLE SHEAVES, ETC.,
MAIN LINE STATION
MARKET STREET CABLE RAILWAY COMPANY, SAN FRANCISCO.

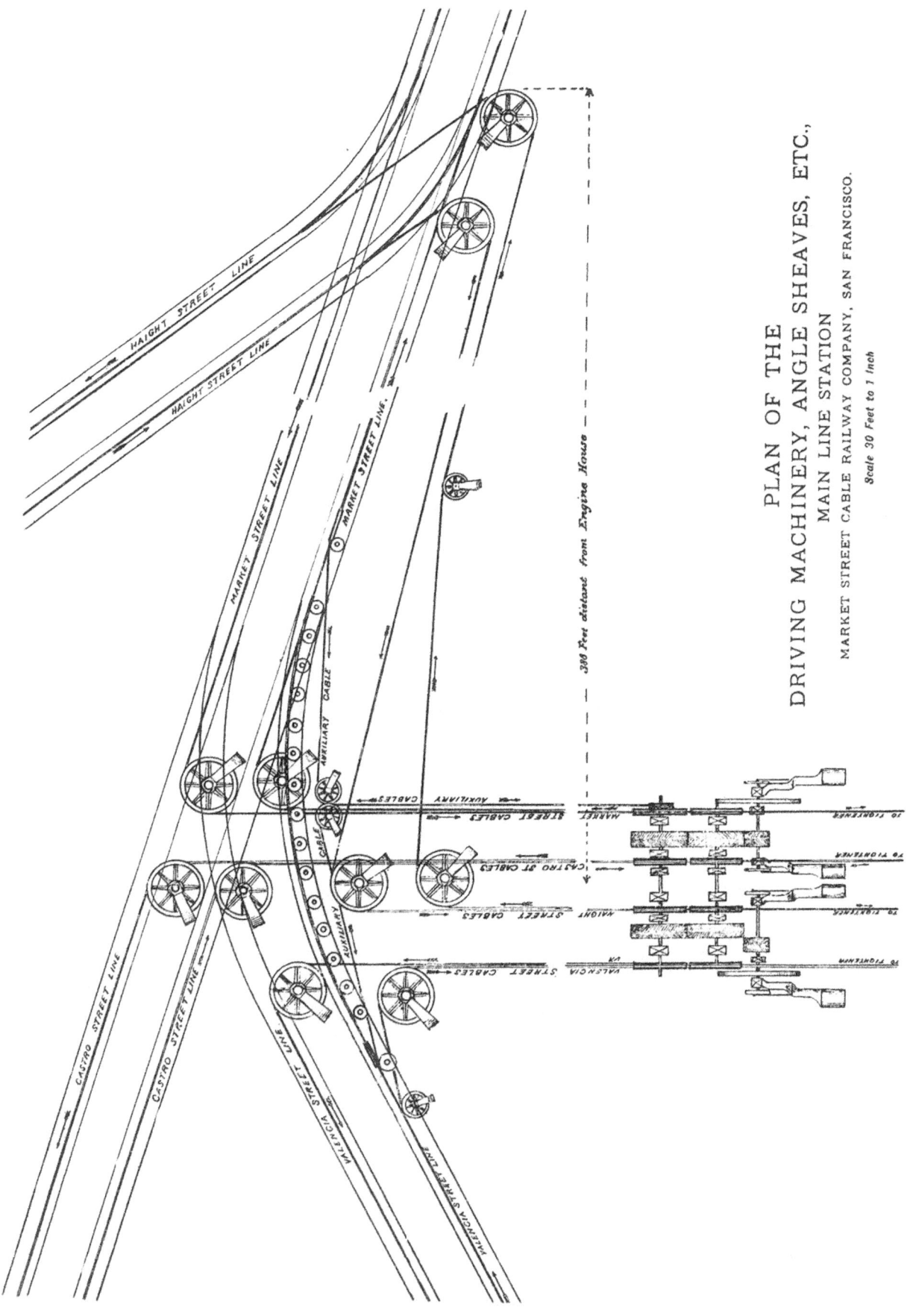

In switching to and from the branch lines, it is necessary to release the cable from the grip while in motion, the car then passing around the curve and switching on to the cable of the other line. In switching from the main to one of the branch lines, in case the cable has not been released by the grip, a safety apparatus, working automatically, closes the switch and compels the car to keep on the main line, when the car is stopped and backed on to the branch line, thus avoiding accident to both grip and cable.

At the termini of the various lines turn-tables 30 feet in diameter, having two sets of tracks laid thereon, are provided for turning the cars and are revolved by the power of the moving cable. At the water-front terminus, where the cars of all the lines concentrate, extra tracks are laid converging into the main track and the cars of the various lines are run upon their respective tracks as the table rotates. The speed of the table at this point is so increased as to meet the dispatch required.

There are three power stations on the lines of this railway. The principal one, located near the junction of the main line with the Valencia Street and Haight Street branch lines, furnishes the power to propel the cables and cars of those lines and has an average of 400-horse power; while the McAllister Street and Hayes Street branch lines have separate power stations near their respective termini, and use 120-horse power for each line.

The Company has about 75 cars on the road ordinarily, but runs out extra cars when required by the traffic.

The various methods and devices used in the construction and operation of this system of cable railways are all covered by the patents belonging to the National and Pacific Cable Railway Companies.

The POWELL STREET RAILWAY is the most recent cable road in San Francisco, and is now in course of construction under the patents of these Companies. It consists mainly of two lines which cross each other at right angles, the Powell Street line, running due north and south, being about $1\frac{1}{2}$ miles in length of double track, and the Jackson Street line, due east and west, $3\frac{1}{2}$ miles of single track, with a parallel line on Washington Street, one block south, 2 miles in length, also single track. The gauge of the road is 3 feet 6 inches, and all the lines will be operated from one engine house or power station near the points of intersection.

The grades on Jackson Street are nearly the same as those on Clay Street, the two streets being parallel, with a distance of only two blocks between them. The greatest elevation on the Jackson Street line is 300 feet above the initial point; and the greatest ascent in one block ($412\frac{1}{2}$ feet) is 65 feet, and on Washington Street 80 feet in one block, or $19\frac{4}{10}$ per 100 feet. On the Powell Street line the greatest elevation is 203 feet, the ascent in three blocks near the summit being respectively 43, 47 and 46 feet in each block.

The CHICAGO CITY RAILWAY COMPANY'S cable line is 17 miles long, all double track, 4 feet $8\frac{1}{2}$ inch gauge. The main line of this road, which was formerly a horse road, has been in operation as a cable line since January, 1882, under patents belonging to the National and Pacific Cable Railway Companies.

The tube in which the rope runs is made deeper than that in San Francisco, being over 4 feet, and the rope is placed about 30 inches above the bottom of the tube. It is especially adapted to snow regions, and the method of its construction is covered by a patent issued to Mr. Henry Root, and among those belonging to these Companies. All the driving and angle pulleys on this road are 12 feet in diameter. On the lines in the heart of the city, the cars move at $8\frac{1}{2}$ miles per hour;

on those from 22d Street south, a mile and a half an hour faster, while on the line beyond the city limits they run at 13 miles per hour. At the town terminus a second rope is employed which is driven by a 6-foot pulley placed on the same shaft as the 12-foot terminal pulley of the main cable, and consequently travels at one-half the speed of the latter, and carries the dummy and cars around three squares, making a return by way of Madison Street, Wabash Avenue and Lake Street to State Street, passing around four corners. The grip is of the lever description. (See Fig. 9.)

The increase of passenger traffic has been so great that one dummy generally hauls two cars, and frequently three, carrying as high as 250 passengers in the train, and 100,000 passengers are sometimes carried in a day. The President of the Company stated at the meeting of the American Street Railway Association held in Cincinnati in October, 1886, that the Company carried last year seventeen millions more people than it did five years before.

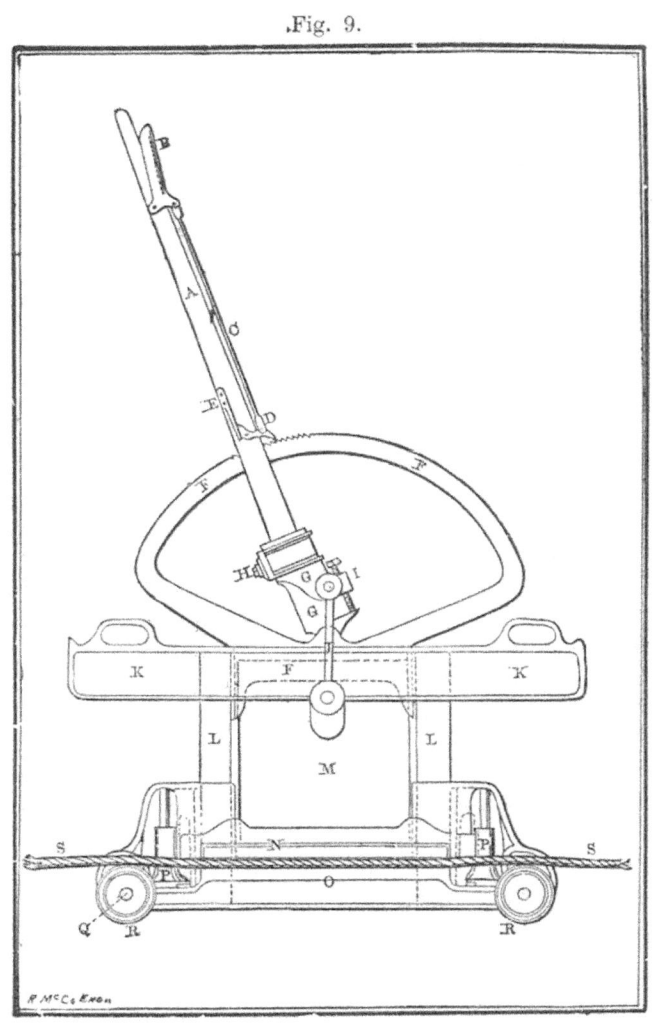

Fig. 9.

GRIP USED ON CHICAGO CITY RAILWAY.

A. Grip Lever. B. Lever Handle. C. Lever Rod. D. Lever Dog. E. Lever Dog Spring. F. Quadrant. Upper G. Adjusting Head. Lower G. Adjusting Shoe. H. Lever Set Screw. I. Adjusting Screw. J. Grip Links. K. Grip Beam. L. Grip Shank. M. Grip Plate. N. Upper Jaw. O. Lower Jaw. P. Spools. Q. Roller Journals. R. Grip Rollers. S. Cable.

The climate of Chicago is one of extremes, the thermometer reaching 90 degrees in summer and 30 degrees below zero-Fahrenheit in winter, and snow falls very heavily. In regard to which the President stated at the meeting that the cable system "has been the best system so far discovered for handling snow. . . . It is a difficult matter to keep our lines free in long continued driving snow storms. After horses have worked all day in the cars and all the next night in the plows, and so on without any rest for three or four days, it is absolute destruction to a very large number of horses, whereas with our cable system we only have to throw in a little more coal to secure the additional power in the engine."

It is the purpose of the Company to extend their cable system over all their main lines, and it is expected that those at a remote distance can be operated at from 12 to 15 miles per hour. The completion of the State Street extension gives a straight line double track cable road 7½ miles long, making the longest continuous cable line in the world. It is operated by four cables.

In LOS ANGELES, CAL., two small cable railways were constructed in the year 1886 under patents belonging to these Companies,—the SECOND STREET CABLE RAILROAD and the TEMPLE STREET CABLE RAILWAY. They are single track roads with turn-outs; one of them being about 6,900 and the other nearly 9,000 feet in length. In operating these roads, where turn-outs are met, the rope is dropped from the grip and the cars pass around the turn-outs by gravitation. There is only one slot for the grip, the rope traveling in opposite directions upon pulleys placed 28 feet apart. The pulleys are constructed in pairs but are not set side by side, one being a foot or two in advance of the other. There is a turntable at each end of the road for reversing the dummy.

These roads were constructed almost entirely in the interest of adjacent property, but have unexpectedly proved to be good investments, and the successful operation of them has led to the introduction of the cable system into that city on a very extended scale.

The LOS ANGELES CABLE RAILWAY COMPANY is now constructing a double track wire-cable railway from the western to the eastern limits of the city, with a branch to the south-east. It will consist of new roads in addition to previously existing horse roads converted into cable lines, embracing over eight miles of double track, and will require three power-stations to operate the system. Additional lines are in contemplation by this Company to the extent of over 50 miles of road, leading to the various suburbs of the city. The road will be built on the plan of the Market Street Cable Railway, under the patents of the National and Pacific Cable Railway Companies, and therefore will be one of the best constructed cable roads in the world. The tracks of the Southern Pacific and other railways will be crossed by viaducts, one of them for a distance of 4500 feet, with stations reached by convenient flights of stairs. In connection with the cable lines there will be an extensive system of short horse-car lines as feeders, which will also be double tracked. The gauge of all the lines will be of the uniform width of three feet six inches, so that in case of sudden increase of travel, horse-cars from the feeders can be coupled to the cable cars and run in trains.

In the City of OAKLAND, CAL., a cable road (the OAKLAND CABLE RAILWAY) was constructed during last year by U. S. Senator Jas. G. Fair under contract for a license for the use of patents belonging to these Companies.

The road runs from the business center of the city on Broadway, along San Pablo Avenue for a distance of about three miles, to the northern boundary of the city.

This road is of the general design of the Market Street Cable Railway of San Francisco, but of lighter materials, and with a gauge of three feet six inches; its cost therefore was less than that of roads intended for heavy traffic, but was well adapted to the purpose for which it was built. The road is double track throughout and has been successfully operated.

In KANSAS CITY the cable system, which has been already applied to four lines of road, is being rapidly extended to street railways which have been hitherto operated by horse-power; and railways on the cable system, either have been built or are now in progress in many other cities, as for instance, PHILADELPHIA, ST. LOUIS, OMAHA, ST. PAUL, MINN., CINCINNATI, PORTLAND, OR., and on the TENTH AVENUE and 125TH STREET RAILROAD in NEW YORK.

In AUSTRALIA the introduction of the cable system has been received with much favor.

The CITY OF MELBOURNE has in operation 15 miles of double-track cable-railway, and 19 miles more are in progress of construction, a portion of which is near completion. Cable railways are being laid on the principal streets in the city, and when completed there will be 34 miles double track, constructed and equipped at a cost of upwards of $5,000,000. The lines already running are operated from six distinct power-stations, which will be increased to nine when the roads now in course of construction are completed.

The CITY OF SYDNEY has one line of cable railway 1¾ miles long, double track, in operation.

In GREAT BRITAIN the wire-cable system has recently been introduced. In the immediate vicinity of LONDON a cable railway about one mile in length (up Highgate Hill) has been constructed and is now in operation. In EDINBURGH, where the gradients are steep, a cable road is being laid down. In BIRMINGHAM, in a portion of the city where the gradients are variable and the curves numerous, a cable road requiring six miles of cable is in course of construction.

MARKET STREET CABLE RAILWAY, SAN FRANCISCO.
VIEW OF MAIN LINE ON MARKET STREET AT ITS JUNCTION WITH GEARY STREET. CABLE CARS OF THE GEARY STREET RAILROAD APPEARING ON THE LEFT

MARKET STREET CABLE RAILWAY, SAN FRANCISCO

VIEW OF MAIN LINE ON MARKET STREET AT ITS JUNCTION WITH McALLISTER STREET, SHOWING McALLISTER STREET BRANCH LINE ON THE LEFT.

Autotype Britton & Rey, S F. MARKET STREET CABLE RAILWAY, SAN FRANCISCO. Inst. Photo. A. P. Flagler, S. F.

VIEW OF MAIN LINE ON MARKET STREET AT ITS JUNCTION WITH HAYES AND LARKIN STREETS, SHOWING CARS ON MAIN AND HAYES STREET BRANCH LINES, A SUTTER STREET RAILROAD ON LARKIN STREET CROSSING MARKET STREET CABLE ROAD AT RIGHT ANGLES.

MARKET STREET CABLE RAILWAY, SAN FRANCISCO.

VIEW OF HAIGHT STREET BRANCH LINE, WITH CARS ASCENDING AN INCLINE OF ONE FOOT IN EIGHT.

Artotype Britton & Rey, S. F.   MARKET STREET CABLE RAILWAY, SAN FRANCISCO.   Int. Photo. A. P. Flagler, S. F.

VIEW OF HAIGHT STREET BRANCH LINE, AT ITS TERMINUS AT GOLDEN GATE PARK, SHOWING CARS ARRIVING, TURNING ON TURN-TABLE AND DEPARTING, AND THE ADAPTABILITY OF COMBINATION CARS FOR RAPIDLY AND SAFELY HANDLING LARGE NUMBERS OF PEOPLE.

Descriptive List of U. S. Letters Patent

BELONGING TO THE

PACIFIC CABLE RAILWAY COMPANY

AND

THE NATIONAL CABLE RAILWAY COMPANY

Parties desirous of obtaining licenses for the construction of Street Railways under the Cable System **WEST** of the 106th degree of longitude, or desiring further information upon the subject, will please address

PACIFIC CABLE RAILWAY COMPANY,

329 Market Street, San Francisco, Cal.

Parties desirous of obtaining licenses for the construction of Street Railways under the Cable System **EAST** of the 106th degree of longitude, or desiring further information upon the subject, will please address

THE NATIONAL CABLE RAILWAY CO.,

140 Nassau Street, New York, N. Y.

These Patents have been issued by the Government of the United States to the following named Inventors or their assignees.

ANDREW S. HALLIDIE, OF SAN FRANCISCO, CAL.

Letters Patent, No. 127,690, bearing date June 11th, 1872,

For Improvement in Griping Pulleys.—This invention consists in joining two clips together by a hinge.

Letters Patent, No. 163,865, bearing date June 1st, 1875,

For Improvement in Endless Rope Traction Ways.—This is an improved automatic closing device, and also an endless chain depression pulley.

Letters Patent, No. 179,016, bearing date June 20th, 1876,

For Improvement in Endless Traction Railways.—Being a switch for transferring grip cars from one track to another.

Letters Patent, No. 179,786, bearing date July 11th, 1876,

For Improvement in Railway Tubes and Cars.—Car wheels without flanges kept on the tracks by means of one or more guide-wheels running in the slot of the tube.

Also for Brake operating in same slot.

Letters Patent, No. 182,663, bearing date Sept. 26th, 1876,

For Improvement in Railways.—Being for a Dummy supporting and carrying the grip adapted to be communicated to passenger cars by an ordinary coupling. This covers the use of a Dummy or Grip car broadly, and has been sustained by the U. S. Courts for the District of California.

Re-issued Letters Patent, No. 7339, bearing date Oct. 10th, 1876. (Original No. 179,086, dated June 20th, 1876.)

For Improvement in Underground Tubes for Propulsion of Cars.—A Tube for underground Cable Railroads having depression pulleys, and openings in the top of tube for withdrawing the grip. Covers broadly the use of depressing pulleys.

Re-issued Letters Patent, No. 7607, bearing date April 17th, 1877. (Original No. 129,130, dated July 16th, 1872.)

For Improvement in Griping Attachments for Ropeways.—This is the first patent ever granted for a griping device for underground Cable Street Railroads, and covers broadly any griping machine adapted to operate through a narrow slot in the street, the operating parts consisting of two or more members, one or more of which is movable and the other stationary, or either having a movement relative to the others, whereby the rope or cable within the tube is seized by the pressure of dies, jaws or rollers upon its surface.

Also covers any griping device adapted to Elevated Cable Railroads having oppositely-moving jaws and rollers.

Letters Patent, No. 195,505, bearing date Sept. 25th, 1877,

For Improvement in Endless Rope Traction Railways.—For a double line of pulleys within a single tube. Also side-bearing pulleys for turnouts.

Letters Patent, No. 276,239, bearing date April 24th, 1883,

For Improvement in Cable Railways.—This is for a Metallic Cellular Covering for a Cable Tube; consisting of cast iron cells filled with wood, asphalt, concrete or other material.

Letters Patent, No. 321,022, bearing date June 30th, 1885,

For Improvements in Endless Rope Traction Railways.—This patent covers broadly a Snow Plow having a griping device attached thereto, adapted to operating through a narrow slot in the street.

Also covers broadly any system of heating pipes within a Cable Tube whereby the snow and ice may be loosened on the track and slot, so as to be removed by a snow plow.

Re-issued Letters Patent, No. 10,681, bearing date Feb. 2d, 1886. (Original No. 330,976, dated Nov. 24th, 1885),

For Improvements in Tramways, for Curves and Cable Grips.—This patent covers broadly any guide-rail or horizontal pulley within the tube; is used on every Cable Road having curves, and is absolutely essential to their operation.

This is one of the controlling patents on Cable Roads.

JOSEPH BRITTON, OF SAN FRANCISCO, CAL.

Letters Patent, No. 181,817, bearing date Sept. 5th, 1876,

For Improvement in Turn-Tables for Endless Traction Ways.—This is for a double-geared Turn-Table.

WILLIAM EPPELSHEIMER, OF SAN FRANCISCO, CAL.

Letters Patent, No. 157,385, bearing date December 1st, 1874,

For Improvement in Endless Rope Traction Railways.—Being a method of constructing a Cable Tube with special drainage facilities. Includes devices for a self-closing slot. Adapted to snow regions.

Letters Patent, No. 160,757, bearing date March 16th, 1875,

For Improvement in Clamp Apparatus for Connecting Street Cars, etc., with Endless Traveling Devices.—Consists of a hydraulic Griping Apparatus, also carrier pulleys for a traveling cable supported on springs.

Letters Patent, No. 166,975, bearing date August 24th, 1875,

For Improvement in Devices for Propelling Cars.—Being for a switch or turn-table, which has a grip chamber extending through it.

Letters Patent, No. 166,976, bearing date August 24th, 1875,

For Improvement in Means for Turning Cars on Short Curves.—Adapted for terminal arrangements where space is limited, and for transferring grip-cars or dummies from one track to another without removing the grip, by means of a slotted tunnel connecting one rope-chamber with another.

Letters Patent, No. 174,358, bearing date March 7th, 1876,

For Improvement in Gripers for Ropeways.—Being the improved Grip in use on the Clay Street Hill, and Presidio and Ferry Railroads in San Francisco.

Letters Patent, No. 189,204, bearing date April 3d, 1877,

For Improvement in Clamps for Endless Rope Railways.—Being a griping device and peculiar arrangement of track to avoid depression pulleys. Adopted on the Geary Street Road in San Francisco.

Letters Patent, No. 193,757, bearing date July 31st, 1877,

For Improvement in Tramway Tracks for Wire-Rope Railroads,—Consists of a method of constructing the road-bed and tube.

Letters Patent, No. 193,939, bearing date August 7th, 1877,

For Improvement in Tightening and Stretching Ropes, Belts, etc.—Being a method of keeping tension on railway cables, etc.

Letters Patent, No. 199,900, bearing date February 5th, 1878,

For Improvement in Tubes for Wire-Rope Railways.—Being a method of construction of track secured to tube of cast-iron, made in sections.

Letters Patent, No. 199,901, bearing date February 5th, 1878,

For Improvement in Wire-Rope Railway Tubes,—Covers a cable railway having two ropes traveling in one tube—the tube being located between the two tracks.

Letters Patent, No. 224,284, bearing date February 10th, 1880,

For Improvements in Wire-Cable Railways.—Being the mode of constructing road-bed, tube and slot, as adopted on the Geary Street Road in San Francisco.

ASA E. HOVEY, OF SAN FRANCISCO, CAL.

Letters Patent, No. 176,136, bearing date April 18th 1876,

For Improvement in Rope-Griping Devices for Propelling Vehicles.—This patent is for a Lever Grip having relatively oppositely-moving rollers or jaws, said jaws or rollers being connected together by a screw bolt, links, or any equivalent adjustable mechanism for taking up the whole of the griping dies or rollers.

It also covers broadly any grip made of a frame, oppositely-moving jaws or rollers, and having the upper edge of the frame made circular and provided with ratchet teeth, and a lever provided with a spring pawl adapted to engage with said ratchet teeth.

Letters Patent, No. 183,928, bearing date Oct. 31st 1876,

For Improvement in Railroad Switches.—Automatic Switch for cable and other street railroads, operated by the wheels of the passing Car or Dummy.

Letters Patent, No. 183,929, bearing date Oct. 31st 1876,

For Improvement in Car Brakes.—This is a wheel brake operated by a lever, and adapted to Cable Dummy or Grip Car.

Letters Patent, No. 184,624, bearing date Nov. 21st, 1876,

For Improvement in Endless Rope Railways.—This patent is for a vibrating depression pulley.

Letters Patent, No. 195,372, bearing date Sept. 18th, 1877,

For Improvements in Endless Rope Traction Railways.—This patent covers the general construction of Cable Railroads:
    1st. Yoke, slot rail, and means of supporting sides of tube.
    2d. Cable tube having continuous channel underneath for drainage.
    3d. Slot rails having smooth vertical surface for guiding grip.
    4th. Depression lever for enabling grip to cross the cable.
    5th. Spring buffer at the terminus of slot.
    6th. Means of lubricating machinery within the tube from outside.

Letters Patent, No. 347,935, bearing date August 24th, 1886,

For Griping Device for Cable Railways.—This covers every detail of what is known as the "Chicago Grip," being the grip now used by the Chicago City Railway Company. A drawing of this grip will be found at page 44, Fig. 9.

HENRY ROOT, of San Francisco, Cal.

Letters Patent, No. 244,147, bearing date July 12th, 1881,

For Tension Apparatus for Cable Railways,—Which provides a means of maintaining an automatic tension on the cable, which can be varied at will; and also a means of taking up the slack by the power of the cable without interfering with the traffic of the road. This tightener is a very *important appliance in the driving-machinery* of cable roads, and is in use on the California Street, Market Street, and Sutter Street cable roads, in San Francisco.

Letters Patent, No. 246,210, bearing date August 23d, 1881,

For Depression Pulley in Cable Roads,—Consists of a vibrating frame carrying a pulley for holding the cable down, and is hinged on an universal joint at the bottom, and so arranged as to be pressed aside to allow the grip to pass.

Letters Patent, No. 246,420, bearing date August 30th, 1881,

For Traction Apparatus for Wire Rope Railways.—This patent is for a car having swivel trucks and a griping device carried by one of the trucks, independent of the car body,—is known as the "Combination Car."

Letters Patent, No. 247,781, bearing date October 4th, 1881,

For Cable Railroad,—Claims a supplemental tunnel beneath and opening into the rope-chamber, forming a receptacle for snow or other substances that may fall through the slot,—is known as "the snow region mode of construction."

Letters Patent, No. 262,126, bearing date August 1st, 1882,

For Construction of Cable Railways.—This patent consists of seven claims:
    1st. For ties, rails and upright support for slot-irons in combination with concrete foundation.
    2d. For track supporting the ties in combination with concrete foundation.
    3d. For combination of rails and a tube formed of concrete or equivalent material.
    4th. For rails and slot-irons, supported and united by the ties in combination with a continuous surrounding mass of concrete or equivalent material, forming a bond and support for the roadway.
    5th. For a structure consisting of rails, slot-irons and connecting ties, consisting of bent bars embracing and supporting the tube.
    6th. For the combined rails, slot-irons and connections, supported by masonry foundation, built to form a tube or part thereof.
    7th. For a tube to receive the rope or cable, made of concrete or equivalent material, open at the top and combined with iron ribs.

This is known as the "Concrete Patent," and was used in the construction of the California Street Railroad, the Chicago City Railway, the Market Street Cable Railway in San Francisco, as also in the re-construction and extension of the Sutter Street Railroad, and in the construction of the cable roads in Kansas City, and on the Tenth Avenue and 125th Street Railroad in New York, besides many other places.

Letters Patent, No. 263,227, bearing date August 22d, 1882,

For an Improved Car for Cable Railroads.—This patent covers broadly any guard or shield carried on the axles without springs, and independent of the car body, and is for the purpose of picking up or throwing off persons or obstructions on the track—is known in Chicago as the "Kid-catcher Patent."

Letters Patent, No. 285,514, bearing date Sept. 25th, 1883,

For Cable Railway,—Covers any curve, operated by an auxiliary cable, adapted to be seized by the same griping device as is used on the main cable.

Letters Patent, No. 286,163, bearing date October 2d, 1883,

For Griping and Carrying Apparatus for Cable Railroads.—This is for a Grip-car or dummy, having a frame for supporting and carrying the grip secured to the axles,—independent of the body which is mounted upon springs, and adapted to carry passengers; also for a griping device, having a fixed frame carrying one jaw and a movable frame sliding upon it carrying the other jaw; and operated by a lever with adjustable cross-head secured to links above the slot—is known as the "Grip Patent."

Letters Patent, No. 304,863, bearing date Sept. 9th, 1884,

For Improved Railway Car.—This is an improved double-truck Cable Car, having an improved rail brake attached to the trucks themselves and operated from the body of the car.

Letters Patent, No. 309,982, bearing date Dec. 30th, 1884,

For Improvement in Tube Structure for Cable Railways.—This is for an improvement in concrete construction of Cable roads, being for piers at short intervals under the body of the road-bed, having their foundation below any ordinary drainage or gas pipes. Also for an improved trap and cover for cable tubes.

Letters Patent, No. 309,983, bearing date Dec. 30th, 1884,

For Improvement in Switching Device for Cable Railways.—This is for a system of safety-switching devices at points where branch lines diverge from the main line of cable roads. Also a cheap and simple means of throwing the cable into the grip at fixed points along the road.

Letters Patent, No. 319,929, bearing date June 9th, 1885.

For Improvement in Cable Railways.—For an auxiliary curve having fast and loose pulleys, whereby the auxiliary cable can be stopped without interfering with the main cable.

Re-issued Letters Patent, No. 10,621, bearing date July 7th, 1885. (Original No. 315,992, dated April 14th, 1885.)

For Improvement in Cable Railways.—This is for a turn-table having two parallel slots extending across it equi-distant from its center of rotation, and a means for turning the table by power derived from the main traveling cable, and covers broadly the combination of a turn-table, a traveling cable and gearing, operated by said cable, whereby the table is rotated.

LELAND STANFORD AND HENRY ROOT, OF SAN FRANCISCO, CAL.

Letters Patent, No. 247,276, bearing date September 20th, 1881,

For Grip Attachment for Cable Railways.—Is a griping device having rollers and opposing dies of wood or other non-metallic substances.

H. ROOT AND F. A. TUCKER, OF SAN FRANCISCO, CAL.

Letters Patent, No. 297,452, bearing date April 22d, 1884,

For Pawl for Cable-Grip Levers.—This is for a pawl having an extension piece adapted by the foot of the gripman so as to disengage the spring pawl and release the grip while the hands of the gripman are otherwise employed. Adopted on the Market Street Cable Railway in San Francisco.

Also for an automatic device for operating the pawl and releasing the grip at fixed points along the road by means of lugs or projections on the top of the slot-bars.

WILLIAM H. PAINE, OF BROOKLYN, N. Y.

Letters Patent, No. 173,329, bearing date Feb. 8th. 1876,

For Improvement in Devices for Connecting Cars with Moving Ropes.—This patent covers broadly all roller grips having rollers or pulleys adapted to seize or grip an endless traveling cable and braking devices by which the rotation of said pulleys or rollers may be checked or retarded.

Letters Patent, No. 296,602, bearing date April 8th, 1884,

For Cable Railway Appliance.—This is an automatic braking device adapted for use on the tension carriages used on cable railways.

Letters Patent, No. 296,603, bearing date April 8th, 1884,

For Auxiliary Switching Apparatus for Cable Railways.—This is for a switching device by which an auxiliary cable is operated in either direction by power derived from the main cable.

Letters Patent, No. 296,604, bearing date April 8th, 1884,

For Griping and Brake Mechanism for Cable Railways.—This is for a griping and brake mechanism adapted to be operated simultaneously by one movement of the operator.

Letters Patent, No. 296,605, bearing date April 8th, 1884,

For Roller Grip for Cable Railways.—This is the latest improved roller grip like that now in use on the New York and Brooklyn Bridge.

Letters Patent, No. 296,606, bearing date April 8th, 1884,

For Automatic Connector and Disconnector for Grips of Cable Railways.—An automatic device adapted for releasing the cable from a horizontal or inclined grip like that used on the New York and Brooklyn Bridge.

Letters Patent, No. 331,237, bearing date Nov. 24th, 1885,

For Cable Supporting Sheave for Cable Railways.—This is an automatic device for raising the endless traveling cable and placing it between the griping jaws or rollers.

Letters Patent, No. 331,238, bearing date Nov. 24th, 1885,

For Hand Mechanism for Operating Gripers for Cable Railways.—Operating mechanism adapted to be used on the front platform of cable cars.

Letters Patent, No. 331,239, bearing date Nov. 24th, 1885,

For Rope-Driving Machinery.—A rope-driving apparatus consisting of a pair of rope-driving drums and an interposed friction drum for transmitting a portion of the power from one to the other.

Letters Patent, No. 371,095, bearing date October 4th, 1887.

For Gripper for Cable Railways.—Covers any roller grip having a braking device and positive jaws, also composite dies or rollers of rubber and other material, also covers any automatic device for compensating for the wear on the dies.

HENRY CASEBOLT, of San Francisco, Cal.

Letters Patent, No. 237,813, bearing date February 15th, 1881,

For Improvement in Grips for Cable-Railroads.—Being the Lever Grip, adapted to drop and pick up the cable at any point along the road.

Letters Patent, No. 237,814, bearing date February 15th, 1881,

For Improvements in the Construction of Cable-Railroads.—Being a method of construction made up of trussed yokes.

Letters Patent, No. 239,726, bearing date April 5th, 1881,

For Improvement in Endless Cableways.—Being a curve for cable railways.

Letters Patent, No. 241,299, bearing date May 10th, 1881,

For Improvement in Switches for Endless Cableways.—Being an improved construction of the tongue formed between the two slots, where tubes branch.

Letters Patent, No. 245,785, bearing date August 16th, 1881,

For a Grip-Operating Device for Cableways.—Consists of a Grip and method of operating the same from the top of the car, by means of rods (inclosed in pipes) passing down through the car.

Letters Patent, No. 249,300, bearing date November 8th, 1881,

For an Improved Cableway.—Being an improved method of construction of road-bed and tube, the yoke being made up of an angle iron truss.

Letters Patent, No. 256,881, bearing date April 25th, 1882,

For Improvements in Underground Cableways.—Being an improved method of guiding the grip *around curves* of cable roads.

Letters Patent, No. 262,640, bearing date August 15th, 1882,

For Improvements in Grip Apparatus for Cableways,—Covers a Griping device under the centre of a street car and so arranged as to be operated from either platform.

ROBERT GILLHAM, of Kansas City, Mo.

Letters Patent, No. 312,624, bearing date February 24th, 1885,

For Carrying Pulley for Cable Railways.—Made in sections and bolted together.

Letters Patent, No. 330,013, bearing date Nov. 10th, 1885,

For Mold for Concrete Tubes for Cable Railways.—This is for a removable mold or core made in two parts, the parts being hinged together and adapted to close together so as to be removed when the concrete has set. Also devices to facilitate moving the molds or cores forward as the work progresses.

Letters Patent, No. 336,561, bearing date Feb. 23d, 1886,

For Cable Railway.—For details of construction; consisting of adjusting strips behind the slot rails, etc.

Letters Patent, No. 345,378, bearing date July 13th, 1886,

For Cable Railway.—For details of construction; consisting of lugs upon a cast yoke and short adjusting rod for adjusting the width of slot. Also openings through a cast yoke adapted to hold the yoke more firmly embedded in concrete.

WM. H. T. HUGHES, of Brooklyn, N. Y.

Letters Patent, No. 134,060, bearing date Dec. 17th, 1872,

For Street Railway Car.—This patent covers broadly any street railway car (horse, cable or electric) having one portion enclosed and the other portion on the same frame open and provided with seats for smokers.

MILTON A. WHEATON, OF SAN FRANCISCO, CAL.

Letters Patent, No. 192,314, bearing date June 19th, 1877,

For Improvement in Car Propellers.— This is for an improved double rope or cable with gripping device for connecting the car or dummy with such double cable, and is the controlling patent in what is known as the "Tom Johnson" system.

THOS. H. DAY, OF SAN FRANCISCO, CAL.

Letters Patent, No. 192,904, bearing date July 10th, 1877,

For Improvement in Griping Device for Rope Tramways.—Consisting of a Griping device, having oppositely-moving top and bottom jaws.

Letters Patent, No. 203,249, bearing date May 7th, 1878,

For Improvement in Rope Tramways and Apparatus.—Providing a *cheap method* of converting a horse-road to the cable system; also further improvements of Griping device.

C. A. GUSTAFSON, OF SAN FRANCISCO, CAL.

Letters Patent, No. 195,504, bearing date Sept. 25th, 1877,

For Improvement in Griping Devices for Traction Cables for Propelling Cars and Vehicles. —An arrangement for throwing the cable out from the grip.

SOLOMON BRISAC AND WM. V. BARBE, OF NEW YORK.

Letters Patent, No. 205,471, bearing date July 2d, 1878,

For Fenders for Cars.—This is for a fender or wheel guard on the side of a car, having openings or doors opposite the wheel boxes or bearing for giving access for oiling, also a hinged semi-circular fender extending around the front of a car.

JOHAN HANSEN, OF SAN FRANCISCO, CAL.

Letters Patent, No. 207,118, bearing date August 20th, 1878,

For Improvement in Gripers for Wire-Rope Railways.—This is for a "winged grip" in which the cable can be dropped and picked up again, whereby the car or dummy is allowed to cross an intersecting cable-road.

Letters Patent, No. 217,096, bearing date July 1st, 1879,

For Improvement in Griping Devices for Wire-Rope Railways.—Being an improvement of the device in the last patent.

JAMES W. C. RHIND, OF SAN FRANCISCO, CAL.

Letters Patent, No. 228,932, bearing date June 15th, 1880,

For Automatic Switch for Wire-Rope Railroads.—This covers broadly any automatic switching device operated by means of a bar or lever, adapted to be moved by the grip shank.

WALTER N. HAWLEY, OF SAN FRANCISCO, CAL.

Letters Patent, No. 230,774, bearing date Aug. 3d, 1880,

For an Improved Street Car.—This is for a Street Car having a passage-way through the center, outwardly facing seats, doors and windows in front of seats.

CHAS. M. CHUBB, OF OAKLAND, CAL.

Letters Patent, No. 235,127, bearing date December 7th, 1880,

For Tramway for Curves and Cable Grips,—Is for a method of guiding and supporting the Grip, in passing curves, without releasing hold of the main cable, by means of guide-rails below the slot and inside of the curved rope-chamber.

SEBRA R. MATHEWSON, OF SAN FRANCISCO, CAL.

Letters Patent, No. 241,044, bearing date May 3d, 1881.

For an Improved Cable Tramway for Carrying Cars Around Curves.—By arranging a series of upright rollers and intermediate plates in the tube, forming a practically continuous surface over which the cable and grip passes.

ALBERT GRÜTTER, OF SAN FRANCISCO, CAL.

Letters Patent, No. 266,029, bearing date Oct. 17th, 1882.

For an Improved Device for Operating Cable Railway Grips.—This is for a combination of a hand-wheel, toothed quadrant, and attachment to a lever-grip, whereby the pressure on the cable can be multiplied to almost any extent.

AIKEN HAMAN, OF SAN FRANCISCO, CAL.

Letters Patent, No. 268,484, bearing date Dec. 5th, 1882,

For Improvement in Fenders or Guards for Wheels of Cars and Dummies.—A device applied to the front of the car, consisting of a padded or spring shield, and a guard for the wheels, the two forming protection for persons struck by the fender or falling under the car at the sides.

Letters Patent, No. 287,377, bearing date Oct. 23d, 1883,

For Improvements in Curves for Cable Railways.—This relates to construction of curves, and devices for carrying the cable around curves, and also construction of griping devices.

JOSEPH JACOBS, OF SAN FRANCISCO, CAL.

Letters Patent, No. 277,490, bearing date May 15th, 1883,

For Wheel-Guard for Railway Cars.—This is for an elastic hinged guard or fender, adapted to extend completely around the front and sides of a car and dummy, together with flexible sectional gates for closing and protecting the opening between car and dummy or grip-car.

Letters Patent, No. 314,580, bearing date March 31st, 1885,

For Wheel-Guard for Railway Cars.—This is for a spring or yielding fender having its outer edge sloping and covered with rubber or other yielding material.

WM. S. RAY, OF SAN FRANCISCO, CAL.

Letters Patent, No. 278,044, bearing date May 22d, 1883,

For Wire-Rope Railway.—This is for an endless chain device, operated by power derived from the main cable, for moving cars over crossings, switches, turntables, etc.

GEORGE DUNCAN, OF NEW ZEALAND.

Letters Patent, No. 295,238, bearing date March 18th, 1884,

For Improvement in Brakes for Cable Railway Cars.—This patent covers the braking of a car by means of a wedge forced into the slot through which the grip shank travels.

Letters Patent, No. 304,262, bearing date Aug. 26th, 1884,

For Improvement in Car-Wheel Locks.—This device is for locking all the wheels of a car or dummy simultaneously by the movement of one lever.

RICHARD K. EVANS, OF WASHINGTON, D. C.

Letters Patent, No. 295,915, bearing date April 1st, 1884,

For Improvement in Griping Device for Cable Ways.—This covers any griping device having dies arranged to be released automatically whenever the strain on them exceeds a certain predetermined amount.

JOHN L. BOONE, OF SAN FRANCISCO, CAL.

Letters Patent, No. 296,916, bearing date April 15th, 1884,

For Improvements in System of Propelling Cars by Means of Cables.—This patent covers broadly any cable road having a duplicate system of cables mounted on pulleys in an underground slotted tube or tunnel, or two separate independent sets of pulleys, one on each side of a perpendicular line drawn through the slot and adapted to be seized by separate griping devices for connecting the car with either cable at will.

GEO. W. BENNETT AND THADDEUS S. FITCH, OF SAN FRANCISCO, CAL.

Letters Patent, No. 299,330, bearing date May 27th, 1884,

For an Improved Pilot or Wheel Guard.—A frame forming a guard in front of the wheels is hung up out of the way when not in use, and a light trigger frame extends in front of it which, when struck by an obstruction on the track, pushes back the guard frame and allows it to fall on the track.

WM. X. STEVENS, OF WASHINGTON, D. C.

Letters Patent, No. 310,331, bearing date Jan. 6th, 1885,

For Hose-Guard for Railways.—This is for a curved passage or tube extending under the ropeway and rails of a cable railway adapted for use of fire-hose, and suitable trap openings outside the rails of the track for giving access thereto, also devices for pulling fire hose through the tunnel or tube without delay.

EGBERT D. HAVEN, OF SAN FRANCISCO, CAL.

Letters Patent, No. 327,083, bearing date September 29th, 1885,

For Improvement in Cable Railways.—The object of this invention is to provide a device by which the cable can be dropped and picked up, and passed over switches and crossings without the aid of switchmen, and without any dips in the grade of the street or bends of the cable.

WILLIAM H. MILLIKEN, OF SAN FRANCISCO, CAL.

Letters Patent, No. 331,902, bearing date December 8th, 1885,

For an Improved Griping Device for Rope Railways.—This consists of a grip which will release the rope to rest it upon the main carrying wheels when required, or which may be withdrawn from the tube without detaching it, or which may be operated from either end of the car while the grip is supported under the car upon the wheel axles, or which will take the rope on either side of its upright shank without turning the grip around, and which will be so compact as to be suitable for a small tube.

CHESTER BULLOCK, OF KANSAS CITY, MO.

Letters Patent, No. 335,560, bearing date Feb. 9th, 1886,

For Double Track Cable Road.—For details of construction of a cable railway, having the tube or tunnel outside the rails of the track.

WM. JAS. THOMAS, OF SAN FRANCISCO, CAL.

Letters Patent, No. 367,467, bearing date Aug. 2d, 1887,

For Cable Railway Grip.—This is for an automatic releasing device, whereby the grip lever is allowed to remain stationery during the release, the movement being effected by means of a slotted hole at the lower end of the links in which the lower cross head is allowed to slide.

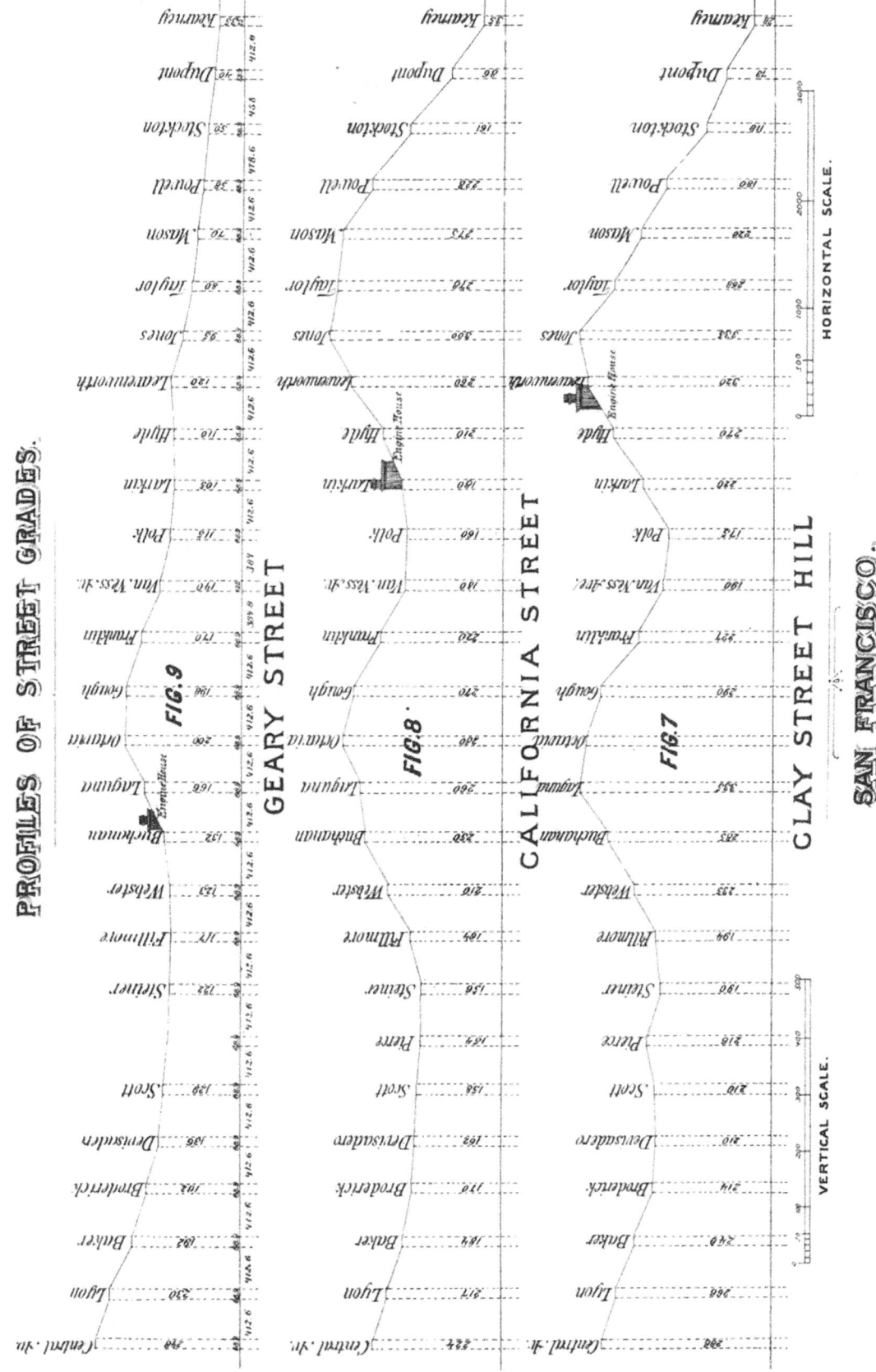

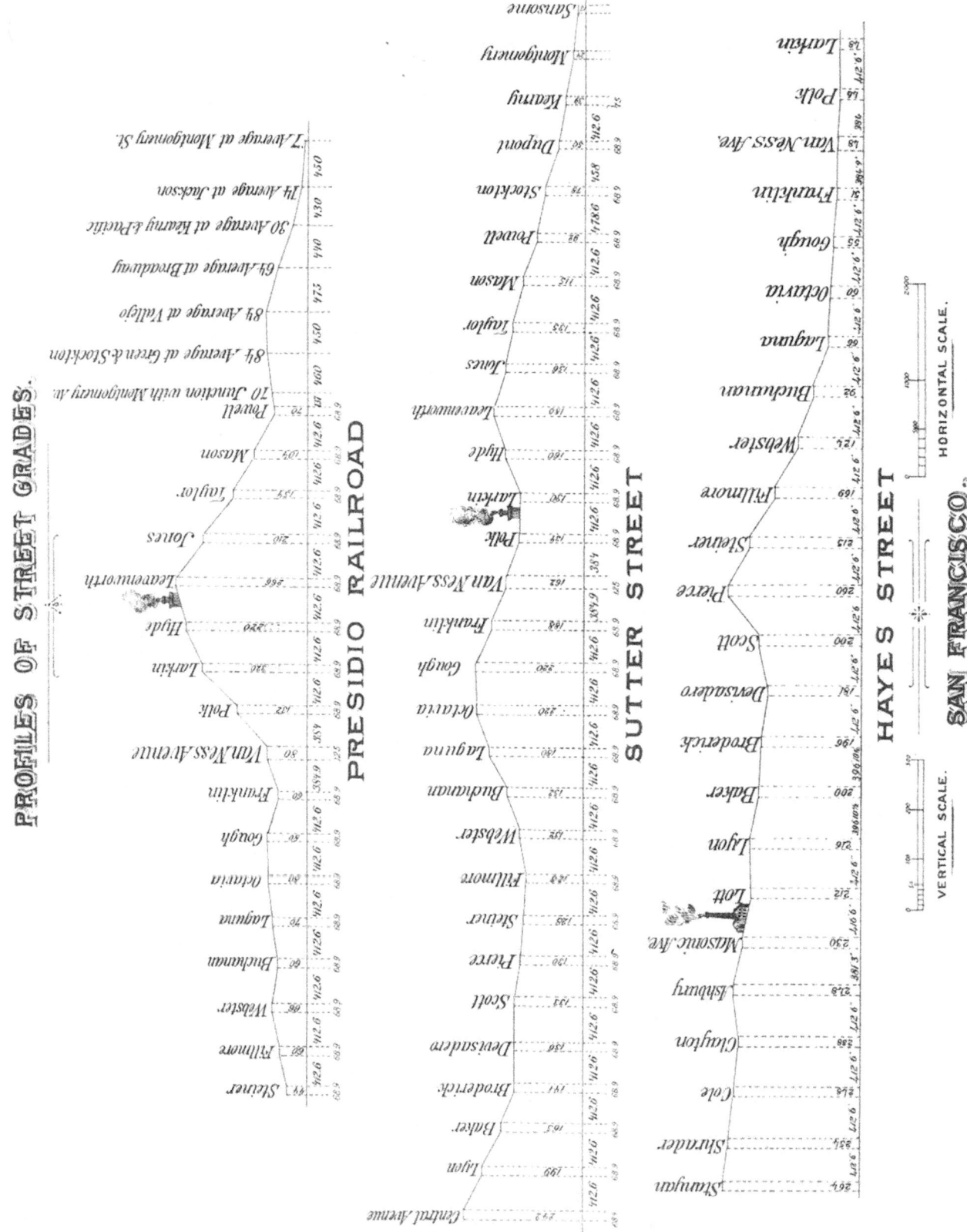

TABULAR STATEMENT CONTAINING INFORMATION AS TO VARIOUS CABLE ROADS IN OPERATION.

NAMES OF ROADS	IN SAN FRANCISCO							IN CHICAGO.	IN LOS ANGELES, CAL.	
	CLAY STREET HILL R. R.	SUTTER STREET R. R.	CALIFORNIA ST. R. R.	GEARY STREET R. R.	PRESIDIO R. R.	MARKET STREET CABLE RAILWAY.	CHICAGO CITY CABLE RAILWAY.	TEMPLE STREET CABLE RAILWAY.	SECOND STREET CABLE R. R.
Commenced operating.	September 1, 1873.	January 27, 1877.	April 9, 1878.	February 16, 1880.	October 23, 1880.	August 22, 1883.	January 28, 1882.	July 14, 1886.	October 14, 1885.
Gauge of road.	3 feet 6 inches.	5 feet.	3 feet 6 inches.	5 feet.	5 feet.	4 feet 8½ inches.	4 feet 8½ inches.	3 feet 6 inches.	3 feet 6 inches.
Length of road, double track.	5,197 feet.	21,090 feet.	12,651 feet.	12,500 feet.	11,000 feet.	12 7/10 miles.	17 miles.	8,725 feet. Single track.	6,940 feet. Single track.
Heaviest grade.	67 feet in 412½.	43 feet in 338.5.	75 feet in 412¾.	38 feet in 412½.	78 feet in 412½.	51 feet in 412½.	Level.	72 feet in 800.	80 feet in 400.
Number of engines employed.	1—1 spare.	4—2 spare.	1—1 spare.	1—1 spare.	1—1 spare.	4—4 spare.	4—2 spare.	One.	One.
Weight of empty car.	2,800 pounds.	4,400 pounds.	4,500 pounds.	4,500 pounds.	4,300 pounds.	Combined, 10,000 lbs.	6,200 pounds.	2,300 pounds.	2,150 pounds.
Weight of empty dummy	2,100 pounds.	3,300 pounds.	4,100 pounds.	4,400 pounds.	4,300 pounds.		6,380 pounds.	2,150 pounds.	2,000 pounds.
Intervals of departure	3 to 5 minutes.	2½ minutes, average.	4 minutes, average	2½ to 4 minutes.	4 to 6 minutes.	2 to 4 minutes.	2 minutes.	10 minutes.	12 minutes.
Average number of round trips per day.	221	253	226	228	210	910	729	96	80
Number of cars and dummies employed.	7 of each.	25 of each.	19 of each.	16 week days. 20 Sundays.	15	70 to 80.	240	6 of each.	6 of each.
Hours run per day	17½	19¼	19	19	17½	20 hours and 40 min.	20	16	16
Number of wire ropes in use.	One.	Three.	Two.	Two.	Two.	Six.	Seven.	One.	One.
Length of ropes used	11,000 feet.	17,900 feet. 16,000 feet. 10,500 feet.	8,840 feet. 17,055 feet.	16,600 feet. 11,300 feet.	12,500 feet. 13,500 feet.	23,958 feet. 21,045 feet. 20,432 feet. 21,702 feet. 5,619 feet. 23,175 feet.	22,920 feet. 4,339 feet. 23,800 feet. 4,969 feet. 23,608 feet. 2,684 feet. 27,800 feet.	18,250 feet.	14,125 feet.
Circumference of wire rope	3 1-16 inches.	3 53-100 inches.	4½ and 4 inches.	3 38-100 inches.	3¼ inches.	4 inches.	4 inches.	3 14-100 inches.	3 14-100 inches.
Speed at which ropes travel.	528 feet per minute	8 and 9 miles per hour.	537 feet per minute	600 and 650 feet per minute.	537 feet per minute	750 feet per minute.	From 8½ to 13 miles per hour.	616 feet per minute	528 feet per minute
Remarks	The engine-house is located on top of the hill, about midway between Polk streets; not on the hill, terminal.	This company has one engine-house, located corner of Sutter and Polk streets; not on the hill.	The engine-house is located in the hollow, 4,220 feet from Kearny St., not on the hill.	The engine-house is situated, 8,000 feet from Kearny street; not on the hill.	The engine-house is located on top of the hill, about midway between terminals.	The principal engine-house is 11,800 feet from the ferry. Two other engine-houses located on branch lines.	The streets are quite level. One engine house is situated about 3 miles, and the other 6 miles from city end of road.	The engine-house is on top of hill, 6,000 feet from city way between end of road.	The engine-house is in valley midway between termini.

TABLES

Of the Comparative Values of Land in San Francisco, California, Showing the Effect of Cable-Railway Construction upon Real Estate in that City.

EXHIBIT No. 1.

Table showing Increase in Value of Real Estate after construction of Cable Street Railways in San Francisco, compiled in the Assessor's Department of said City, in the year 1885.

Name of Railway Co.	Date of franchise or commencement of work on railroad.	Value of land bordering on the lines of route the year previous to construction.	Value of land for the year 1884, showing increase.	Percentage of increase in value.	Remarks.
Clay Street Hill	1873	$ 775,740	$1,089,365	40.42	Always cable.
Sutter Street	1876	1,189,990	1,410,125	18.49	Changed from horse to cable in 1876.
California Street	1876	1,707,415	2,979,736	23.82	Always cable.
Geary Street	1878	1,431,430	1,548,615	8.18	Always cable.
Presidio and Ferries	1879	519,880	624,055	20.03	Always cable.
Market Street	1879	23,309,495	26,801,265	14.98	Changed to cable in 1883.

The above are the assessed values for the years given of lands bordering within about 200 feet of each side of railway line. The territory lying beyond said 200-foot line, though participating in benefit of cable railway facilities, is not included, as it is not needed for demonstration.

WASHINGTON BARTLETT,
Mayor.

LOUIS F. HOLTZ,
Assessor.

EXHIBIT No. 2.

Table showing Depreciation in Value of Real Estate along routes traversed by Horse-car Street Railways in San Francisco, compiled in the Assessor's Department of said City, in the year 1885.

Name of Railway Co.	Value of land bordering on the lines of route for the year 1879.	Value of land for the year 1884, showing depreciation.	Percentage of depreciation in value.	Remarks.
Omnibus	$16,147,270	$12,125,755	33.16	Always used horses.
North Beach and Mission	9,530,200	7,265,205	31.17	Always used horses.

The year 1879 was taken as a date for the first year, as the one least unfavorable to the horse-car system. Had the dates of construction been taken, the difference in "percentage of depreciation" would have been greatly increased.

NOTE: The Omnibus is the oldest horse-car railway line in the city, and was established about the year 1862. The North Beach and Mission is the next oldest line, and was established within a year of the Omnibus.

WASHINGTON BARTLETT,
Mayor.

LOUIS F. HOLTZ,
Assessor.

CHICAGO CITY RAILWAY.

CONVERTED FROM A HORSE-ROAD TO THE CABLE SYSTEM IN 1881.

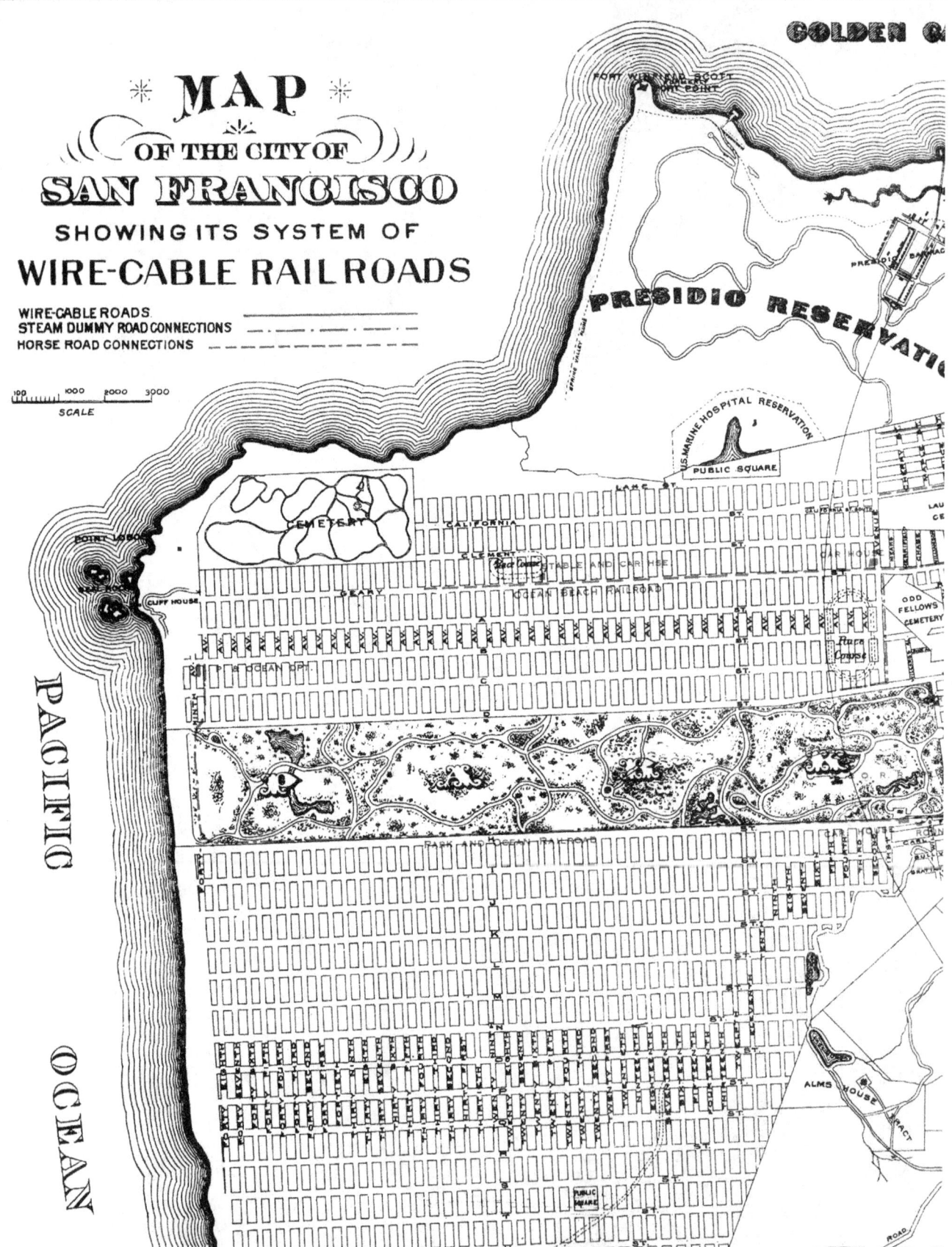

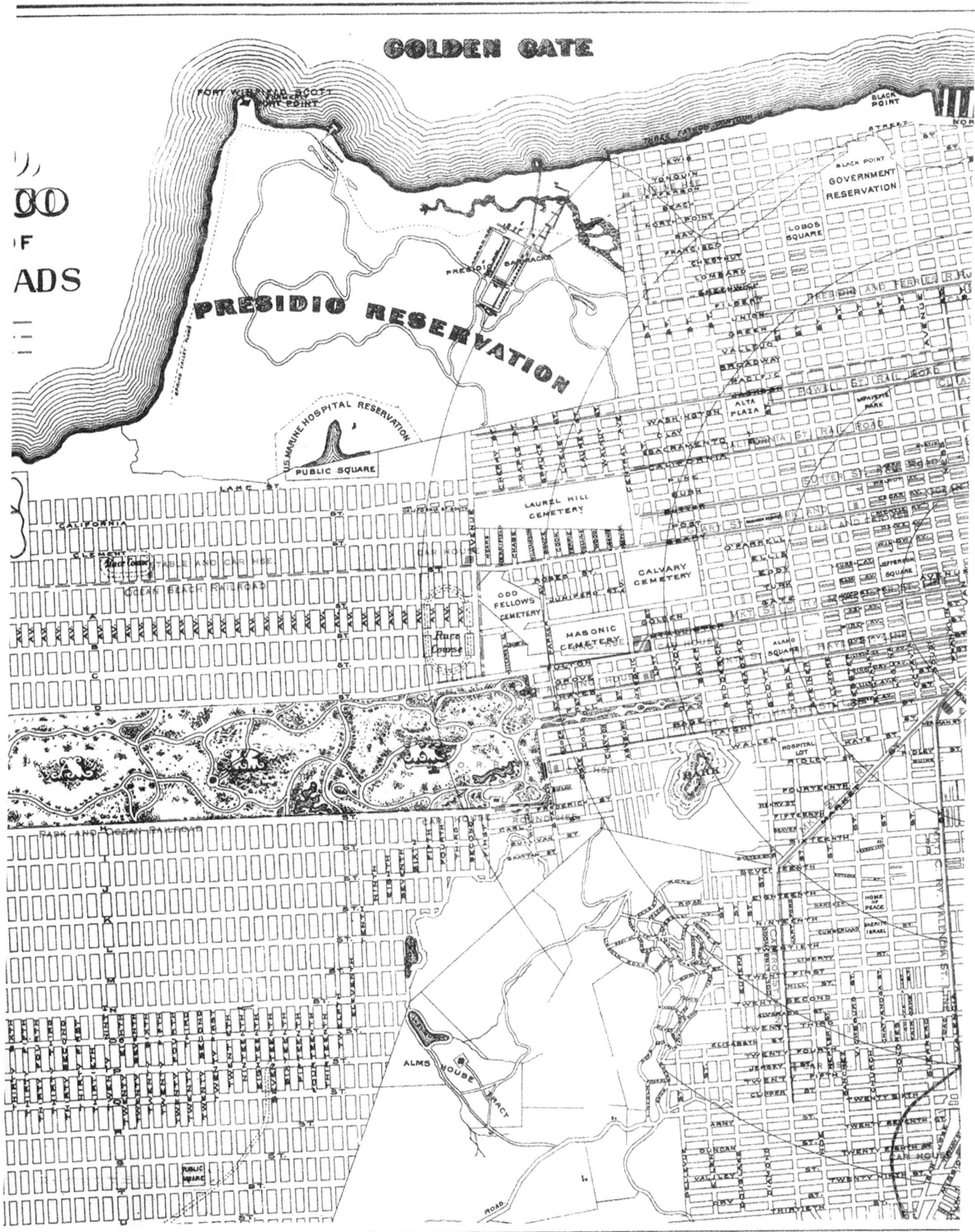

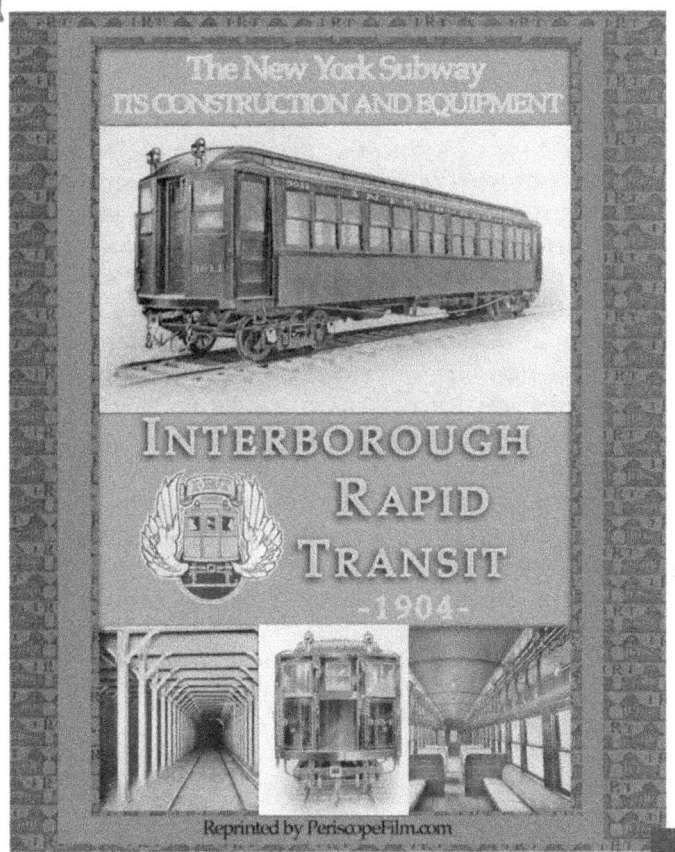

On October 27, 1904, the Interborough Rapid Transit Company opened the first subway in New York City. Running between City Hall and 145th Street at Broadway, the line was greeted with enthusiasm and, in some circles, trepidation. Created under the supervision of Chief Engineer S.L.F. Deyo, the arrival of the IRT foreshadowed the end of the "elevated" transit era on the island of Manhattan. The subway proved such a success that the IRT Co. soon achieved a monopoly on New York public transit. In 1940 the IRT and its rival the BMT were taken over by the City of New York. Today, the IRT subway lines still exist, primarily in Manhattan where they are operated as the "A Division" of the subway. Reprinted here is a special book created by the IRT, recounting the design and construction of the fledgling subway system. Originally created in 1904, it presents the IRT story with a flourish, and with numerous fascinating illustrations and rare photographs.

Originally written in the late 1900's and then periodically revised, A History of the Baldwin Locomotive Works chronicles the origins and growth of one of America's greatest industrial-era corporations. Founded in the early 1830's by Philadelphia jeweler Matthais Baldwin, the company built a huge number of steam locomotives before ceasing production in 1949. These included the 4-4-0 American type, 2-8-2 Mikado and 2-8-0 Consolidation. Hit hard by the loss of the steam engine market, Baldwin soldiered on for a brief while, producing electric and diesel engines. General Electric's dominance of the market proved too much, and Baldwin finally closed its doors in 1956. By that time over 70,500 Baldwin locomotives had been produced. This high quality reprint of the official company history dates from 1920. The book has been slightly reformatted, but care has been taken to preserve the integrity of the text.

NOW AVAILABLE AT
WWW.PERISCOPEFILM.COM

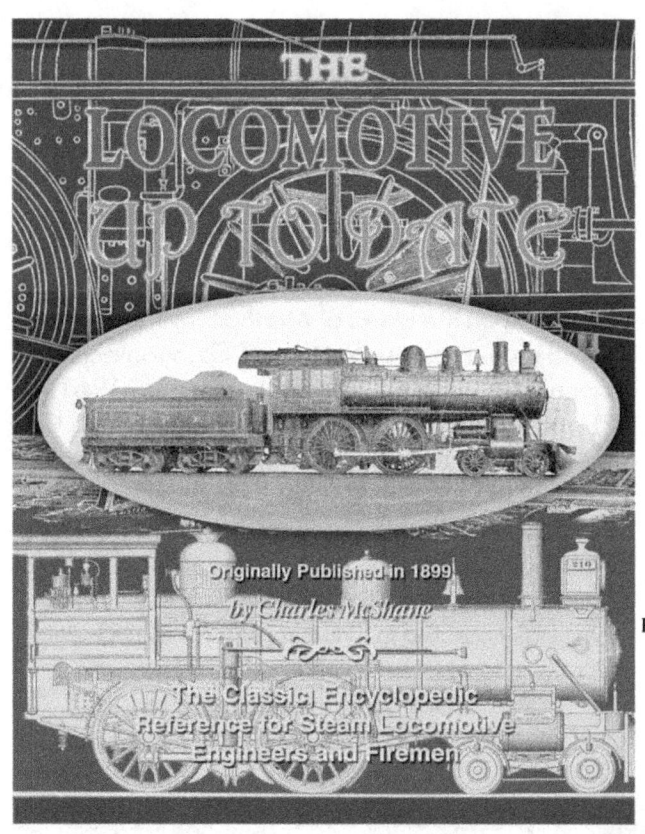

When it was originally published in 1899, **The Locomotive Up to Date** was hailed as "...the most definitive work ever published concerning the mechanism that has transformed the American nation: the steam locomotive." Filled with over 700 pages of text, diagrams and photos, this remains one of the most important railroading books ever written. From steam valves to sanders, trucks to side rods, it's a treasure trove of information, explaining in easy-to-understand language how the most sophisticated machines of the 19th Century were operated and maintained. This new edition is an exact duplicate of the original. Reformatted as an easy-to-read 8.5x11 volume, it's delightful for railroad enthusiasts of all ages.

Originally printed in 1898 and then periodically revised, **The Motorman...and His Duties** served as the definitive training text for a generation of streetcar operators. A must-have for the trolley or train enthusiast, it is also an important source of information for museum staff and docents. Lavishly illustrated with numerous photos and black and white line drawings, this affordable reprint contains all of the original text. Includes chapters on trolley car types and equipment, troubleshooting, brakes, controllers, electricity and principles, electric traction, multi-car control and has a convenient glossary in the back. If you've ever operated a trolley car, or just had an electric train set, this is a terrific book for your shelf!

ALSO NOW AVAILABLE FROM PERISCOPEFILM.COM!

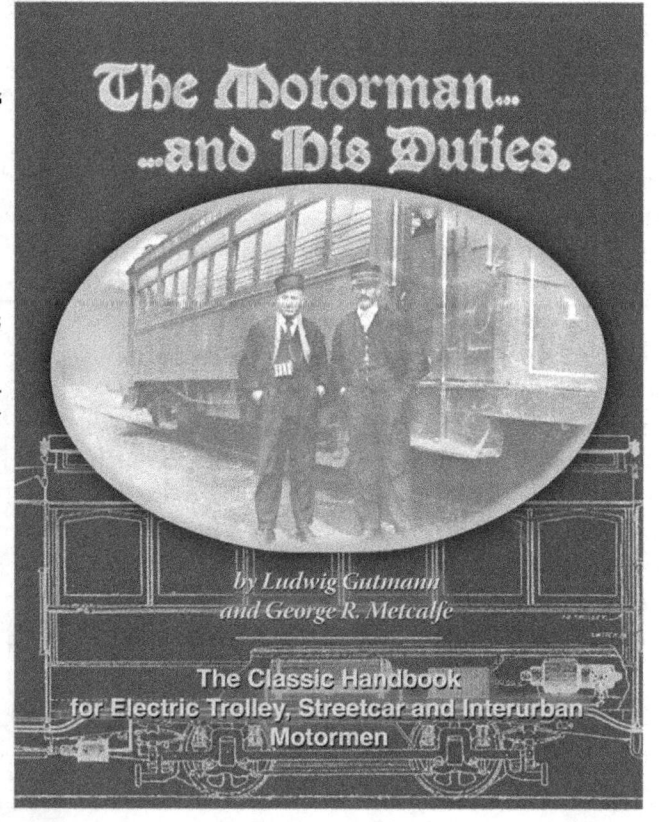

THE CLASSIC 1911 TROLLEY CAR BUILDER'S REFERENCE BOOK

ELECTRIC RAILWAY DICTIONARY

By Rodney Hitt
Associate Editor, Electric Railway Journal

REPRINTED BY PERISCOPEFILM.COM

©2007-2010 Periscope Film LLC
All Rights Reserved
ISBN #978-1-935700-16-6
www.PeriscopeFilm.com

www.ingramcontent.com/pod-product-compliance
Lightning Source LLC
LaVergne TN
LVHW061346060426
835512LV00012B/2590